ETHICAL RISK MANAGEMENT:

Guidelines for Practice

William F. Doverspike, PhD

Professional Resource Press
Sarasota, Florida

Published by Professional Resource Press
(An imprint of Professional Resource Exchange, Inc.)
Post Office Box 15560
Sarasota, FL 34277-1560

The copy editor for this book was Brian Fogarty, the managing editor was Debra Fink, the production coordinator was Laurie Girsch, and the cover was designed by Carol Tornatore.

Library of Congress Cataloging-in-Publication Data

Doverspike, William F., date.
    Ethical risk management : guidelines for practice / William F.
Doverspike.
        p.   cm.
    Includes bibliographical references and index.
    ISBN 1-56887-057-4 (alk. paper)
    1. Mental health personnel--Decision making--Moral and ethical
aspects. 2. Mental health personnel--Professional ethics.
3. Informed consent (Medical law) 4. Risk management. I. Title.
RC455.2.E8D68   1999
174'.2--dc21   99-28460
                                                          CIP

ISBN-13: 978-1-56887-057-1
ISBN-10: 1-56887-057-4

ACKNOWLEDGMENTS

I wish to thank my colleagues in the Georgia Psychological Association (GPA), particularly those serving on the Ethics Committee, for their support and encouragement over the years.

I especially thank my colleagues Ted Ballard, PhD, Tom Friedrichs, PhD, and Linda Scott, PhD, for being role models who encouraged me to strive for an aspirational level of ethical behavior. I thank Rob Remar, Esquire, for providing valuable legal consultations which provided a foundation for my interests in ethical risk management. I thank David Doverspike, Esquire, and the Honorable Robin Nash for helping me learn to do the next right thing in ethical decision making. I thank my friend and advisor, Craig Mullins, for encouraging me to put my ideas into writing.

I thank George Taylor, PhD, for the opportunity to teach my first ethics class, an experience which changed the direction of my career. I thank my students at the Georgia School of Professional Psychology (GSPP) for asking questions that have inspired me to improve my knowledge of ethics.

PREFACE

When I was invited to become a member of my state association's Ethics Committee, I agreed to do so after learning that the committee's role was to become more educative and less adjudicative in its functions. At my first committee meeting, I quickly and pleasantly rediscovered that the vast majority of my colleagues were careful, conscientious, and compassionate in their work. If you are reading this book, you are probably a member of that vast majority. If you regularly consult with colleagues about what you are doing, you are definitely one of those careful and conscientious practitioners.

I was also surprised and somewhat perplexed to learn that the most serious ethical violations could have been avoided had the psychologist simply observed the most *basic* ethical principles, and followed the most basic guidelines such as "always practice within your area of competence" and "maintain clear boundaries." In cases alleging less-serious complaints, the practice of "consulting with a colleague" and "keeping current with standards" seemed particularly relevant. In situations involving unfounded complaints, a well-documented record was always the best defense.

As I began to review more and more cases, I was impressed with how often the same ethical principles applied to different situations. I began to compile a list of some practical guidelines based on these observations. Most of these guidelines are not ethical principles per se but are simply common-sense strategies for putting ethics into practice. These practical guidelines suggest what to do rather than what not to do. In providing consultations to colleagues facing complex situations in which no single course of ethical action seemed clear, I began to understand the importance of using a problem-solving or decision-making model in applying ethical standards to specific situations. Finally, when reviewing office procedures of colleagues who seemed to aspire to ethical excellence, I developed a greater appreciation for the use of informed consent procedures which help prevent ethical problems before they arise. Incorporating some of these practical guidelines and decision-making models into your practice patterns may offer you a greater degree of protection while you offer your patients a higher standard of care. Remember, when you protect your client, you protect yourself.

William F. Doverspike, PhD, ABPP
Atlanta, Georgia
July, 1999

TABLE OF CONTENTS

ETHICAL
RISK
MANAGEMENT:

Guidelines for Practice

ETHICAL RISK MANAGEMENT: SOME PERSONAL REFLECTIONS

Dear Dr. [Professional's Name]:

On [Date] your State Association Ethics Committee received a complaint against you from [Complainant]. The complaint has been assigned to one of the Committee's investigative panels. The panel is charged with determining whether sufficient cause exists for the complaint to be formally docketed with the Committee.

Enclosed please find a copy of the completed Ethics Complaint Form and all materials submitted by [Complainant], a copy of the *Ethical Principles* which [Complainant] claims are at issue, and a copy of the Committee's Rules and Procedures.

Please file a response within 45 days of receipt of this letter. If you need additional time, the panel will consider extending the time to respond for good cause if a written request to extend the time is made within 45 days of receipt of this letter.

We request that you respond to the complaint personally and in writing. Please be as complete as possible. You are, of course, free to consult with legal counsel but your response should be from you and not from a third party acting on your behalf. You are responsible for any legal expenses incurred. Please understand that all information submitted by you shall become a part of the record in this matter and could be used if any further proceedings ensue.

We recognize that receiving a complaint is stressful and unpleasant even if the complaint is without merit. If you have any questions or concerns, please do not hesitate to contact the undersigned directly.

Sincerely yours,

[Committee Member]

Known in one state as the "Notice to Complainee of Investigation" (Georgia Psychological Association [GPA], 1996, p. 11), some variation of the form letter* on the preceding page might be your first notice that an ethics complaint has been filed by a former client. Now that I have your attention, I would like to introduce you to a practical handbook which addresses ethics from a risk-management perspective. Using personal observations written from a first-person perspective, I will provide an informal discussion of some practical guidelines designed to help colleagues integrate ethical principles into their clinical work.** The text is based on a series of articles which originally appeared in the *Georgia Psychologist* magazine (Doverspike, 1996a, 1996b, 1997a, 1997c, 1999b) and *Innovations in Clinical Practice* (Doverspike, 1995, 1997b, 1999a).

UNDERSTANDING ETHICAL
AND LEGAL STANDARDS

Sometimes we err without realizing what we are doing, only later to learn that ignorance of the law is a poor defense. Perhaps the place to start is with your profession's *Ethics Code* itself, since such codes are often incorporated into the statutory laws of many states. A good rule of thumb is to be sure you have copies of your profession's *Ethics Code* and your state licensing board's *Code of Conduct* so that these can be consulted from time to time. When confronting an ethical dilemma, just refreshing your memory by reviewing relevant standards can help improve your ethical decision-making process. If a single relevant standard applies in a particular situation, then your first question should be, "Is there a reason to deviate from the standard?" (Haas & Malouf, 1995, p.

---

* Reprinted with permission from the Georgia Psychological Association.

** Although the principles contained in this book are applicable to all mental health professionals, the author acknowledges that psychologists, psychiatrists, social workers, marriage and family therapists, and professional counselors have different *Ethics Codes* and specialty guidelines which they follow. This book is not intended to provide legal advice and the information contained in it should not be relied upon for legal advice. The reader is encouraged to contact a qualified attorney for legal advice regarding state laws governing professional conduct.

12). For those interested in maintaining the highest standard of care, consider reading one of the commentaries on the *Ethics Code*. Several ethics books for psychologists, including *Ethics for Psychologists* (Canter, Bennett, Jones, & Nagy, 1994) and *Ethical Conflicts in Psychology* (Bersoff, 1995), are included in the References section of this book.

Consider having lunch with a respected colleague and discussing a section of the *Ethics Code* that is relevant to your common areas of practice. Have a *scenario-based* discussion rather than a *procedure-based* conference. In other words, rather than taking an ethical principle and discussing all the situations in which it may apply, try taking a potentially problematic situation and discussing all of the ethical principles that may apply. Ask questions. What are the differences between privacy, confidentiality, and privileged communication? How do you obtain informed consent from a patient whose competence is in question? Does an authorization for release of information always have to be in writing? How much information does a managed care client require in order to give informed consent? Should you fax requested information to an insurance company to obtain payment of a claim? Who owns and controls the privilege of a deceased person's records?

Clinicians interested in improving their ethical decision-making abilities may also be interested in consulting the Canadian Psychological Association (CPA) *Code of Ethics for Psychologists, Revised 1991,* which contains a decision-making model. The Canadian model includes several steps which typify ethical decision making, including identification of relevant issues and practices, development of alternative courses of action, analysis of likely risks and benefits of each course of action, and evaluation of the results of the course of action. The Canadian model is discussed in greater detail in the Ethical Decision Making chapter of this book.

OBTAINING ADEQUATE
INFORMED CONSENT

Informed consent has become an increasingly important concept as clinicians have become more aware of evolving ethical standards and relevant case law (Bennett, Harris, & Remar, 1996).

In an age of litigation, it is important to remember that "psychologists can be held liable for failure to obtain appropriate informed consent *even if their subsequent treatment of the patient is exemplary from a clinical perspective*" (Stromberg & Dellinger, 1993, p. 5). In the practice of managed care, informed consent has become an even greater concern as case managers and utilization reviewers require disclosure of information that may result in a reduction of benefits or a limitation in the number of treatment sessions that are authorized.

Ethical issues relevant to informed consent are addressed in the American Psychological Association (APA; 1992) *Ethical Principles of Psychologists and Code of Conduct* which in part states that, "Psychologists obtain appropriate informed consent to therapy or related procedures, using language that is reasonably understandable to participants" (p. 1605).* Although the specific content of informed consent may differ in each situation, there are some basic elements which provide a foundation for understanding informed consent. According to APA standards, "Informed consent generally implies that the person (1) has the capacity to consent, (2) has been informed of significant information concerning the procedure, (3) has freely and without undue influence expressed consent, and (4) consent has been appropriately documented" (p. 1605).

The process of informed consent should involve ongoing communication, clarification, and decision making (Pope & Vasquez, 1991). In keeping with the spirit of this process, clinicians have a duty to determine (informally or otherwise) whether the patient is competent to give informed consent or whether the situation may justify some type of service in the absence of fully informed consent. When a patient is legally incapable of giving informed consent, the provider must obtain informed permission from a legally authorized person, if such substitute consent is permitted by law. In addition, the provider must inform the patient about the proposed interventions, seek the patient's assent to those interventions, and consider the patient's preferences and best interests. For a competent person who is fully capable of giving consent, the provider must consider whether the patient has been

---

*Ethical Principles of Psychologists and Code of Conduct is copyrighted by the American Psychological Association. This and other excerpts are reprinted with permission.

provided with the relevant information to make an informed decision and whether the patient sufficiently understands the information. As a final consideration, the provider must determine whether the patient can provide consent on an adequately voluntary basis. Because treatment is an ongoing process, the patient must adequately understand and voluntarily agree to any changes in the ongoing treatment plan. Consent issues addressed during the tenth session of psychotherapy may be very different from those addressed during the initial interview. Haas and Malouf (1995, p. 62) describe informed consent as a process, "perhaps beginning with more general and global descriptions of the elements of treatment and later progressing to specific descriptions of specific procedures as needed."

Informed consent considerations take on even greater significance with the use of more invasive or innovative procedures. From a risk-management perspective, it is interesting to note some of the provisions of the *Psychologist's Professional Liability Insurance Policy* administered by the American Psychological Association Insurance Trust (APAIT). APAIT-insured psychologists who offer services "involving physical contact with clients" are required to submit a written explanation including "the percent of clients receiving physical contact and a copy of the release form" (APAIT, 1996, p. 2). As a general rule, the more invasive or innovative the procedure, the greater the need for adequately informed consent and careful documentation of procedures (Doverspike, 1997b, 1999a). Because adequate informed consent procedures are so important in helping to prevent ethical problems before they arise, such procedures are discussed in greater detail in a separate chapter on Informed Consent Issues.

Whether one chooses a more casual question-answer format or a formal, written, narrative approach to obtaining informed consent, compliance with the APA ethical standard requires that the patient's consent be "appropriately documented." Most proponents (Bennett, Harris, & Remar, 1995, 1996, 1997; Harris & Remar, 1998; Schlosser & Tower, 1991; Younggren, 1995) advocate the use of a signed, detailed, and well-documented informed consent procedure. Consent forms should reflect, but should never replace, the ongoing dialogue between clinician and patient. Those interested in an aspirational standard of care should consider the use of a combined verbal discussion and written documentation approach which "provides persuasive evidence that a conscientious effort to obtain informed consent was made" (Stromberg et al., 1988, p. 451).

PRACTICING WITHIN YOUR
AREA OF COMPETENCE

Not everyone can handle the rigorous requirements for working with dissociative patients or performing child custody evaluations. Knowing when to refer to another practitioner is as important as knowing when to treat. As Canter et al. (1994) point out, "Merely having an interest in a particular area does not necessarily qualify one to practice in that area" (p. 34). In my own practice, although I am board certified in neuropsychology, I routinely refer *child* neuropsychological evaluations to other neuropsychologists. Similarly, although I provide numerous consultations for memory testing, I never perform "recovered memories" testing. As a general rule, ethical problems are less likely to arise when practicing within one's area of competence. However, an exception to this rule may apply to specialists who have become overly comfortable *within* their area of competence, such as the neuropsychologist who finds "a little brain dysfunction" in almost anyone, the eating disorders therapist to whom everyone looks "a little bulimic," or the educational specialist who is eager to diagnose "ADD" (the popular acronym which has seemingly replaced careful examination of the diagnostic criteria for Attention-Deficit/Hyperactivity Disorder). To use an old diagnostic observation, it's easier to see what you know than it is to know what you see. The ethical implication of this observation is that a careful and conscientious clinician is always alert to evidence that may not support his or her initial intuitive impressions.

Practicing *outside* an area of competence can be especially tempting in the practice of managed care. Many closed provider panels have few, if any, psychologists in certain specialties. A patient may get a provider's name from an "800" number or a referral directory with little or no understanding of the provider's limitations. If you do not know your limitations, you will be overcome by them. Again, knowing when to refer is as important as knowing when to treat. One survey revealed that almost 25%

of psychologists reported that they had either "rarely" or "sometimes" provided services outside their areas of competence (Pope, Tabachnick, & Keith-Spiegel, 1987). It may be helpful to remember the advice, "Know what you know, and know what you *don't* know."

If you decide to practice in an area beyond the boundaries of your competence, it is especially important to obtain case consultation or ongoing supervision. Specific standards for education, training, and supervised experience are established for areas of practice where it is recognized that specialized training and expertise are necessary to be competent. Examples for psychologists include *Specialty Guidelines for Forensic Psychologists* (Committee on Ethical Guidelines for Forensic Psychologists, 1991), *Standards for Neuropsychologists* (Reports of the INS – Division 40 Task Force on Education, Accreditation, and Credentialing, 1987), and *Guidelines for Child Custody Evaluations in Divorce Proceedings* (APA, 1994). For proposed standards in emerging fields such as geropsychology, see the literature by Moye and Brown (1995). Clinicians practicing in emerging specialty areas for which recognized standards do not yet exist should take reasonable steps to ensure competence and to protect others from harm.

Competence is not only a concern for those undergoing supervision – it is a prerequisite for those *providing* supervision. Clinicians providing supervision to others need to be aware that supervision involves considerable responsibility and needs to be taken seriously. One rule of thumb is, "Do not supervise what you cannot do" (Bennett et al., 1995, 1996, 1997). Supervisors should also be "well trained, knowledgeable, and skilled in the practice of clinical supervision" (Stoltenberg & Delworth, 1987, p. 175). Because supervisors assume the ultimate responsibility for all of their supervisees actions, high-risk areas of practice require special consideration during supervision. Examples of high-risk situations include supervisee boundary violations with patients, treatment of life-endangering patients, and the use of memory retrieval techniques with adult survivors of childhood abuse (Knapp & Vande-Creek, 1997). Koocher and Keith-Spiegel (1998) have pointed out that lack of timely feedback "is at the root of many ethical complaints that grow out of supervisory relationships" (p. 324). Documentation of supervisory sessions should reflect the quality of care given to the patient, as well as the quality of supervision provided to the supervisee (Bridge & Bascue, 1988; Knapp & VandeCreek, 1997).

BEING AWARE OF CHILD CUSTODY EVALUATIONS

Although child custody evaluations were mentioned in the preceding section on practicing within one's area of competence, this specialty stands apart from others because it is a major area in which ethics complaints against psychologists occur. Over the past several years, state licensing boards have received an increasing number of complaints related to this litigious area (H. T. Ballard, personal communication, February 24, 1997; Bennett et al., 1997). In some states, custody evaluators can expect to have professional liability complaints routinely filed against them by noncustodial parents (Harris & Remar, 1998).

The greatest risks seem to occur with clinicians who do not have extensive training and experience in this area. Although a therapist may have good intentions, serious consequences can be caused by errors in judgment or in failing to be aware of the many pitfalls in performing custody evaluations. For example, it would be considered unethical for a clinician to conduct a custody evaluation involving a family with whom the clinician has a current or prior therapeutic or other conflicting relationship (Morris, 1997). Although clients may be forgiving of the lapses on the part of a well-liked therapist, the same clients may not be forgiving of the lapses made by a custody evaluator who writes a report contrary to their interests.

Because we live in a culture which "permits everything and forgives nothing" (Shapiro, 1994), clinicians who perform custody evaluations should be aware of the associated risks. Proficiency in conducting custody evaluations requires competence in several areas, including child development, psychological assessment, family system dynamics, and forensic testimony. Clinicians performing custody evaluations should be familiar with the *Guidelines for Child Custody Evaluations in Divorce Proceedings* (APA, 1994). Particularly when practicing in a high-risk specialty area involving litigation, the usual and customary risk-management considerations (such as obtaining informed consent and documenting one's decisions in writing) take on even greater significance.

USING PROJECTIVE
RETROSPECTIVE THINKING

Before you take action in a situation, try to *anticipate* possible consequences of your actions and *think* how your actions will be viewed later if you have to explain them to a colleague. In cognitive-behavioral psychotherapy, this strategy is known as "consequential thinking." In addictive disease relapse prevention, it is called "thinking the drink through." In professional liability risk management, it is called "projective retrospective" thinking (Bennett et al., 1996; E. Harris, personal communication, April 22, 1996). In other words, think forward (projectively) and then look back (retrospectively) on your work. A colleague once jokingly told me, "If you can't explain it to your mother, you shouldn't be doing it." Another good rule of thumb is to not do anything that you would not want to explain to a peer review committee.

Project yourself into the future, and then think how you would look back on your actions if you were to be retrospectively evaluated. Even better, when writing your notes, think how your actions will later look to someone reading them. Think how your actions will sound to your patient's attorney in court. If you think your rationale and decisions sound good in your office, think how they will sound if you have to explain them in court.

CONSULTING WITH A COLLEAGUE

From time to time, everyone faces situations which require special consideration beyond one's own best judgment. The wise practitioner knows when to identify those situations that deserve consultation with a peer. Peer consultation means talking with a respected colleague who is impartial, objective, and knowledgeable. It does *not* mean talking to someone who will simply agree with whatever actions you have already taken. A good peer is someone who can help you see your ethical blind spots. If you are not sure who to call, one option is to call your local professional association and request an *ethics inquiry* or case consultation. Two heads are usually better than one and a brief consultation is better than none.

Good motives can sometimes lead to bad results. Sooner or later, everyone faces a situation in which one's best efforts may result in adverse consequences. In such situations, the best defense is to have obtained and documented peer consultation. Such documentation will at least demonstrate careful consideration of appropriate standards of care. Peer consultations are particularly important when clinicians are faced with situations in which the clinician must consider actions in high-risk situations (e.g., dispensing with informed consent, involuntarily committing a suicidal client, breaching confidentiality in a duty-to-protect situation, performing child custody evaluations, terminating with a noncompliant client).

While there are some ethicists who advise clinicians to "consult on every case" (Pope, 1989a), this strategy can be difficult at best. If you *don't* consult on every single case, here's another strategy that can sometimes help: Visualize your most respected colleague sitting in the consultation room with you and your patient. While picturing your colleague in front of you, think to yourself, "What would *he* or *she* do? What would *he* or *she* say?" If you're *still* not sure, you should *definitely* consult with a peer.

DOCUMENTING YOUR DECISIONS IN WRITING

Remember the old documentation rule, "If it wasn't written, it wasn't done." It is not only important to document what you *did*; it is also important to document what you *didn't* do. Get in the habit of making contemporaneous notes, including date of entry. In retrospective review, your notes are your best (and sometimes only) evidence that you have been a careful and conscientious clinician. In situations involving unfounded complaints, a well-documented record is always the best defense. A psychologist who had been investigated by a state licensing board called me to express his frustration with the absence of due process in which the investigator would not reveal the name of the complainant or the specific nature of the complaint. The psychologist lived in a state in which the licensing board was not required to inform the psychologist of the specific nature of the complaint. I suggested that the psychologist consult with an attorney, request from the state board the name of the patient who had filed the complaint, and then obtain the patient's permission to release that file to the licensing board. Several months later, after the licensing board had closed the case as frivolous, I asked the psychologist how he had managed to defend himself against a complaint that was never revealed to him. He simply smiled and said, "I just gave them my notes, and I had *lots* of notes."

On almost every occasion when I have obtained legal consultation, one bit of advice I can always expect to hear is to "put it in writing." Adequate record keeping provides the first indication to attorneys that your treatment meets minimum standards of care. I've gotten to the point where I not only "put it in writing," but I often imagine the patient's attorney reading my notes as I write them. It has been suggested that clinicians "hallucinate on their shoulder the image of a hostile prosecuting attorney who might preside at the trial in which their records are subpoenaed" (Gutheil, 1980, p. 481). In discussing the client record as a tool in risk management, Piazza and Yeager (1991) recommend that psychologists "not write anything in the client's records that you would not want a client's lawyer to read" (p. 344). As a general rule, write your notes the way you would like to read them in court. Even better, as one hospital attorney has advised, "Write your notes the way you would like someone *else* to read them in court" (J. D. Doverspike, personal communication, November 1, 1996).

Gutheil (1980, p. 479) suggests that clinicians "use paranoia as a motivating force" in writing progress notes and keeping effective records for forensic purposes, utilization review, and good treatment planning. While minimum requirements for record keeping are contained in statutory law and various accreditation guidelines, there are no maximum standards for record keeping. In other words, "There is a floor, but no ceiling, on what to write" (Gutheil, 1980, p. 480). The *General Guidelines for Providers of Psychological Services* (APA, 1987) recommend that case notes minimally include dates and types of services as well as any "significant actions taken" (p. 717). Ideally, notes should also include a summary of topics discussed, techniques or interventions employed during the session, and the patient's reaction. In order to minimize subjectivity or unsupported impressions, any clinical impressions should be supported by behavioral observations.

On a more aspirational level of record keeping, for each significant patient-therapist treatment decision, the record should include (a) what the choice is expected to accomplish, (b) why the clinician believes it will be effective, (c) any risks that might be involved and why they are justified, (d) what alternative treatments were considered, (e) why they were rejected, and (f) what steps were taken to improve the effectiveness of chosen treatment (Soisson, VandeCreek, & Knapp, 1987). In other words, document what you did and why you did it, but also document what you didn't do and why you didn't do it (Stromberg et al., 1988). Gutheil (1980, p. 482) recommends that the clinician "think out loud in the record" so that one's notes reflect active concern for the patient's welfare and consideration of various interventions. Gutheil emphasizes, "As a general rule, the more uncertainty there is, the more one should think out loud in the record" (p. 482).

MAINTAINING CLEAR
BOUNDARIES WITH PATIENTS

A colleague on an ethics committee once said that the single best way to avoid the most serious ethics complaint was to "never have sex with a patient." One might add: "or a former patient." This advice may seem so obvious that it doesn't need repeating, yet this issue concerns the most serious ethical breach of our profession. Sexual impropriety accounts for approximately half of the costs of malpractice cases and over 20% of the total number of claims (Pope, 1989b; Pope & Vasquez, 1991; Stromberg & Dellinger, 1993). Gabbard and Pope (1988) have documented the many harmful effects of "professional incest." In almost every complaint of sexual misconduct there are also other boundary violations as well. Even if the allegations of sexual misconduct cannot be proven, the boundary violations can almost always be proven. When boundary violations begin to occur, a clinician may start sliding down the slippery slope toward sexual misconduct. Although a mandatory ethical obligation would be to "never have sex with a patient," a more aspirational standard would be to "maintain clear boundaries with patients." By way of analogy, everyone knows that a driver shouldn't fall asleep at the wheel while driving. Although some people do fall asleep, the warning line should not be "don't fall asleep at the wheel," but rather "don't drive when you are tired."

What's the difference between a psychiatrist and psychologist? A psychiatric colleague once joked to me that the difference was that psychologists "have to wait 2 years before having sex with their patients." Although his comment reflected a distorted view of the American Psychological Association standard, my psychiatric colleague and I agreed that "once a patient, *always* a patient." In other words, there is no such thing as a "former patient." In reviewing the results of their national survey of psychiatrists' attitudes concerning sexual intimacies with their patients, Herman, Gartrell, Olarte, Feldstein, and Localio (1987) point out that the concept of a so-called "posttermination waiting period" before sexual intimacies are initiated is naïve because it disregards both the continued inequity of roles of the therapist and former patient, and the "timelessness of unconscious processes" (p. 168). It is significant to note that the current psychiatric version of the *Principles of Medical Ethics* (American Psychiatric Association, 1993) includes the following statement, "Sexual activity with a current or former patient is unethical" (§2.1). Legislatively oriented clinicians should be reminded of the exemplary leadership which was provided by Florida psychologists in this regard. State of Florida Chapter 21U-15.004 states, "For purposes of determining the existence of sexual misconduct as defined herein, the psychologist-client relationship is deemed to continue in perpetuity." It may be helpful to remember that mental health professionals have other continuing responsibilities and obligations to patients (e.g., maintaining confidentiality and protecting privilege) which are not affected by the "passage of time after termination" (Gabbard & Pope, 1988, p. 23). Because a client always has the right to renew a professional relationship in the future, one must assume that a professional relationship continues to exist as long as the client assumes that it does, regardless of the amount of time that has elapsed in the interim (Gottlieb, 1993).

It may be helpful to clarify a common misunderstanding regarding the so-called "waiting period" of 2 years. Some psychologists seem to believe that APA *Ethical Principles* (1992) give a "green light" to sexual involvement with former patients 2 years after the termination of psychotherapy. This is not true. APA *Ethical Standard* 4.07 states that "The psychologist who engages in such activity after the two years following cessation or termination of treatment bears the burden of demonstrating that there has been no exploitation" of the former patient (p. 1605). The prototype given in the APA debates over this section of the code dealt with the hypothetical psychologist who might meet a former client in a social situation many years after having conducted one session of career counseling with the person. Although scenarios of such "unusual circumstances" might be possible, they are indeed rare and clinicians can get themselves into trouble if they start thinking of patients as potential romantic partners. Although the 2-year period has been described as a "flashing red light," the author's opinion is that it should be viewed as a stop sign on a dead end street.

The prohibition of sexualized dual relationships may also extend to persons with whom the patient has "an affectionate personal relationship" (Pope, 1986, p. 25). The most current version of the *Psychologist's Professional Liability Policy* administered by the American Professional Agency and issued by the American Home Assurance Company (AHAC; 1990) includes special provisions which limit coverage for any claims of sexual involvement "with or to any former or current patient or client of any Insured, or with or to any relative of or member of the same household as any said patient or client, or with or to any person with whom the patient or client or relative has an affectionate personal relationship" (p. 3). As emphasized by Pope (1986), actual erotic, physical contact need not be present because included in the provisions of the AHAC policy is any "attempt thereat or proposal thereof" (p. 25). Pope further pointed out that proposals or attempts at erotic, physical contact need not actually occur but need only be "alleged at any time" (p. 25). Clearly, the rule of thumb is to avoid even the *appearance* of impropriety, which means setting clear limits and exercising firm boundaries from the first session onward.

KEEPING COMMUNICATION
CHANNELS OPEN

In the practice of medicine, it has often been said that one of the best ways to avoid a malpractice lawsuit is to maintain open communication while treating the patient with kindness and respect. Mistakes happen and people are usually more forgiving when their doctor has had an ongoing open and honest relationship with them. Kovacs (1984) has suggested that, "Those who are involved in meaningful dialogues are not likely to sue each other" (p. 12). In the early years of my hospital practice, I once witnessed a "shotgun" malpractice suit in which several physicians were named in the lawsuit yet one physician was unexpectedly spared the ordeal (Doverspike, 1997a, 1999a). The patient later disclosed that the one physician who was spared had done his best to treat her with respect, keeping communication open during a difficult involuntary hospitalization. Similarly, I have known both psychologists and psychiatrists whose communication skills have allowed them to identify and resolve major violations before those rose to the level of formal complaints. On the other hand, I have also had patients tell me that they had filed complaints against their physicians because "my doctor never talked to me." In listening to these stories and in consulting with physicians over the years, I have been reminded repeatedly how important it is to keep communication channels open.

A forensic psychologist once estimated that 95% of malpractice complaints could be prevented by "treating your patient with respect and kindness and as a person from whom you can learn a great deal" (Sutton, 1986). In my own experience, I have found that conflicts with patients can usually be minimized or avoided altogether by discussing concerns at the outset. When conflicts do arise, discussing the issue first is usually the best path towards successful resolution. I am often surprised by the number of patients who say that they had not discussed their concerns with their therapist before filing a complaint. Client dissatisfactions that are addressed at the source rarely rise to the level of formal complaints. Because we are in the business of communicating with others, it makes sense to use communication as a cornerstone of ethical practice management.

Remember that there is no such thing as a frivolous complaint. Given the amount of time and the enormous emotional (and often financial) resources required to resolve formal complaints, it is important to take all patient dissatisfactions seriously. A good working relationship with your patient may help guarantee that the patient will report dissatisfactions directly to *you* rather than to someone else. In the event that your patient makes a complaint directly to you, the best course of action would be to take the complaint seriously, discuss the patient's concerns, obtain consultation with a peer, work towards a satisfactory resolution, and document your actions in writing. Of course, the exception to this rule would apply in the unfortunate event that, if a lawsuit happens to arise, the clinician would be advised to cease communicating with the patient and begin consulting with an attorney.

ASPIRING TO A STANDARD
OF EXCELLENCE

Mark Twain (1901) once said, "Always do right. This will gratify some people, and astonish the rest." This wisdom reflects an important risk-management strategy for ethical responsibility. In discussing the characteristics of the ethically responsible professional, Van Hoose and Paradise (1979) outline four conditions, suggesting that a professional "is probably acting in an ethically responsible way concerning a client if (1) he or she has maintained personal and professional honesty, coupled with (2) the best interests of the client, (3) without malice or personal gain, and (4) can justify his or her actions as the best judgment of what should be done based upon the current state of the profession" (p. 58).

Psychologists interested in an aspirational level of ethical awareness might be interested in reviewing literature such as *Ethics for Psychologists* (Canter et al., 1994) and *Ethical Conflicts in Psychology* (Bersoff, 1995), which contain practical case discussions, empirical research, and scholarly commentaries related to various ethics topics. Counselors interested in achieving excellence in ethical aspirations might be interested in reviewing the *American Counseling Association (ACA) Ethical Standards Casebook* (5th ed.) (Herlihy & Corey, 1996).

SUMMARY OF ETHICAL RISK-
MANAGEMENT CONSIDERATIONS

As a member of a state association ethics committee, I have personally observed that ethics committees often spend hours upon hours deliberating the merits of complaints that could have been avoided altogether had the psychologist simply spent 15 minutes consulting with a colleague in the first place (Doverspike, 1997a). In situations involving unfounded complaints, a well-documented record is always the best defense. A clinician's best, ethical risk-management strategy includes understanding relevant ethical and legal principles, utilizing an ethical decision-making plan, obtaining adequate informed consent, practicing within an area of competence, treating the patient with respect and kindness, keeping communication channels open, obtaining peer consultation on a regular basis, and documenting the record as if the patient's attorney were reading it. It may be instructive to remember the words of Barnett (1997) who noted, "Too often I have experienced that sinking feeling in the pit of my stomach when reviewing an ethics complaint, seeing how costly this is to the individuals involved and often how easily it could have been avoided" (p. 20). As a general rule of thumb, it is easier to avoid a complaint than it is to defend one.

POINTS TO REMEMBER

- Understand ethical and legal standards. When in doubt, read the manual.

- Always obtain adequately informed consent.

- Practice within your area of competence.

- Beware of child custody evaluations.

- Use "projective retrospective" or consequential thinking.

- Consult with a colleague. Two heads are better than one.

Continued ➡

- Document your decisions in writing.

- Maintain clear boundaries with clients and former clients.

- Keep communication channels open with your patient.

- Aspire to a standard of ethical excellence.

- Remember it is easier to avoid a complaint than it is to defend one.

ETHICAL DECISION MAKING: DOING THE NEXT RIGHT THING

Psychologists striving for the highest standard of care may be interested in reviewing some of the literature on ethical problem-solving and decision-making models. An underlying assumption regarding ethical decisions is that they are based on *principles*. Under ideal conditions, one should be able to specify the principles upon which an action is based. A cornerstone of good ethical decision making includes *knowledge* of applicable ethical standards. One's knowledge of standards should include an understanding of the difference between *mandatory* and *aspirational* ethical obligations. Aspirational obligations represent ideals or the ethical "ceiling" of behavior while mandatory requirements represent minimal standards or the "floor" of ethical behavior (Haas & Malouf, 1995, p. 4). Aspirational ethical obligations represent the highest ideals of excellence embodied in the six general statements contained in the APA (1992) *Ethical Principles of Psychologists*, while *mandatory* requirements represent the enforceable ethical standards delineated in the more specific *Ethical Standards* or *Code of Conduct*. For purpose of clarity throughout this text, the term *Ethical Principles* is used to refer to the six *General Principles*, while the term *Ethical Standard* is used to refer to specific standards contained in the *Code of Conduct*.

In learning to identify mandatory requirements, it may be helpful to consult the official ethical standards of one's profession. Because mandatory ethical standards are incorporated into statutory laws in many states, one should also be familiar with regulatory laws governing practice in one's state. For example, Georgia psychologists should be familiar with the Georgia *Code of Conduct* (*Georgia State Board of Examiners of Psychologists, Laws,* August 31, 1997; *Georgia State Board of Examiners of Psychologists, Rules,* March 9, 1999). Those interested in a more aspirational level of ethical awareness might be interested in reviewing literature such as *Ethics for Psychologists* (Canter et al., 1994) and *Ethical Conflicts in Psychology* (Bersoff, 1995), which contain practical case discussions, empirical research, and scholarly commentaries related to various ethics topics.

Although knowledge of ethical principles and codes of conduct provide a guide for aspirational and mandatory behavior, reliance only upon ethical standards may be open to criticism because such standards can be interpreted to suit the occasion (Tymchuk, 1986). Furthermore, because there are many practical situations which are not clearly addressed by specific ethical standards, there is often a need for some guide to ethical decision making. As Herlihy and Corey (1996) point out, "When we find ourselves navigating in waters that are not clearly charted by our profession's ethical codes, we must be guided by an internal ethical compass" (p. 11). One such "internal ethical compass" may involve a set of decision-making rules by which ethical principles can be applied to practical situations.

The APA (1992) *Ethical Principles of Psychologists and Code of Conduct* are intended to provide "both the general principles and the decision rules to cover most situations encountered by psychologists" (p. 1599). The Preamble offers the following guidelines:

> The development of a dynamic set of ethical standards for a psychologist's work-related conduct requires a personal commitment to a lifelong effort to act ethically; to encourage ethical behavior by students, supervisees, employees, and colleagues, as appropriate; and to consult with others, as needed, concerning ethical problems. Each psychologist supplements, but does not violate, the Ethics Code's values and rules on the basis of guidance drawn from personal values, culture, and experience. (p. 1599)

Although the APA Preamble contains some guidelines for "the development of a dynamic set of ethical standards," the *Ethical Principles* do not contain a formal decision-making model. In their commentary on the APA *Ethics Code*, Canter et al. (1994) describe a seven-step decision-making process which emphasizes *knowledge* of ethical standards, state and federal laws and regulations, and institutional rules and regulations. The seven steps are as follows: "(1) Know the Ethics Code, (2) know the applicable state and federal laws and regulations, (3) know the rules and regulations of the institution where you work, (4) engage in continuing education in ethics, (5) identify when there is a potential ethical problem, (6) learn the skills needed to analyze ethical obligations in often complex situations, and (7) consult with senior professionals knowledgeable about ethics" (p. 3). The authors devote little attention to the skills needed to resolve complex ethical dilemmas. Although Canter et al. acknowledge that there are "numerous systems for formal analysis and resolution of ethical problems and dilemmas" (p. 6), the authors conclude that a detailed discussion of such systems is beyond the scope of their book.

A review of the literature indicates that several formal decision-making models have been developed (Eberlein, 1987; Haas & Malouf, 1995; Hill, Glaser, & Harden, 1995; Keith-Spiegel & Koocher, 1985; Kitchener, 1984; Koocher & Keith-Spiegel, 1998; Sinclair, Poizner, Gilmour-Barrett, & Randall, 1987; Tymchuk, 1986). The common features of these models include a sequential decision-making process involving identification of the affected parties and ethical principles involved in the decision, consideration of alternatives, choice of appropriate actions, and evaluation of consequences. Ethical decisions may be made rapidly in many situations although more time-consuming, careful deliberation may be required in more complex situations. Relatively quick decisions can usually be made in situations in which there are clear-cut standards which do not conflict with each other. More careful consideration may be required in more complex situations in which there are ethical principles that conflict with each other. In such situations, consultation with a colleague can increase one's objectivity in the ethical decision-making process.

Kitchener's (1984) model provides an example of a relatively simple, two-step decision-making process related to moral judgments. Kitchener describes two levels of moral thinking: an immediate intuitive response, and a critical-evaluative level of thinking. The *intuitive* level represents ordinary or perhaps impulsive moral judgments which include the "shoulds" and "musts" of morality. The *critical-evaluative* level is comprised of three components which include rules and codes, ethical principles, and ethical theory. When considering conflicting values, rights, and responsibilities in a particular situation, the ethically conscientious practitioner may modify or qualify his or her immediate intuitive response on the basis of critical-evaluative thinking, even though the initial response may be ethically acceptable.

Gottlieb's (1993) model provides an example of a decision-making process applied to a specific topic – avoiding exploitive dual relationships. The model is based on three dimensions which are considered important in relationships. The first dimension is *power*, which refers to the power differential which a psychologist may have in relation to a client. The second dimension involves *duration of the relationship*, which is an aspect of power because it is assumed that power increases over time. The third dimension involves *clarity of termination*, or the likelihood that the psychologist and client will have professional contact at some point in the future. The decision-making process involves examination of the contemplated relationship as opposed to the current professional relationship with respect to each of these dimensions. Gottlieb encourages clinicians to consult with colleagues and examine both relationships for role incompatibility before proceeding with the contemplated relationship.

The Canadian Psychological Association (CPA; 1991) *Code of Ethics for Psychologists, Revised 1991* is one of the few professional codes which contains a formal decision-making model. Based on models proposed by others (Sinclair et al., 1987; Tymchuk, 1986), the Canadian model outlines several steps which typify the ethical decision-making process. The following outline summarizes the ethical decision-making model based on the Canadian *Code of Ethics*, with each section representing one of the steps contained in the model. In providing some commentary and discussion of each of these steps, I have integrated ideas from decision-making models proposed by other writers (Canter et al., 1994; Haas & Malouf, 1995; Keith-Spiegel & Koocher, 1985; Kitchener, 1984; Koocher & Keith-Spiegel, 1998). I have also relied heavily on Haas and Malouf's (1995) text *Keeping Up the Good Work.*

AN ETHICAL
DECISION-MAKING MODEL

Identifying the Affected
Parties Involved

The first step in making a decision involves identifying the individuals or groups that need to be considered to arrive at a solution to the ethical dilemma (Sinclair et al., 1987). Haas and Malouf (1995, p. 9) use the term *stake-holders* to refer to those parties who have legitimate stakes in the outcomes of a situation. Although traditional stake-holders included the therapist and the client, legitimate stake-holders may also include significant others, those who are likely to be affected by the situation, and other parties who contract or pay for services. Like good treatment planning, good decision making involves consideration of the preferences of others, particularly in terms of rights and responsibilities involved. Koocher and Keith-Spiegel (1998) recommend that the clinician evaluate the rights, responsibilities, and welfare of all affected parties. Sinclair et al. recommend that clinicians "take each of these individuals/groups in turn and explain in detail what consideration each is owed and why" (p. 6).

Identifying Ethically
Relevant Principles

When confronting an ethical dilemma, refreshing one's memory by reviewing relevant standards can help improve one's ethical decision-making ability. Relatively quick decisions can usually be made in situations in which there are clear-cut guidelines or standards which do not conflict with each other. There are many occasions in which what initially appears to be an ethical problem turns out to be a procedural or technical problem. For example, choice of assessment instruments in a psychological test battery would usually be considered a *technical* rather than an ethical decision. However, choosing to administer psychological tests to one but not both parents in a child custody evaluation would involve an ethical decision-making process.

If a single relevant standard applies in a particular situation, one's first question should be, "Is there a reason to deviate from the standard?" (Haas & Malouf, 1995, p. 12). If there is no single ethical principle that applies to the situation, one's next step would involve identifying the relevant ethical dimensions that make the issue problematic.

Developing Alternative Courses of Action

There are some situations in which no single ethical dimension seems to outweigh the others. In such situations, a "solution-generating" or "brainstorming" approach can be helpful and a variety of actions may prove to be ethically appropriate (Haas & Malouf, 1995, p. 15). In generating possible courses of action, one should consider a variety of actions regardless of whether such actions initially appear to be ethically appropriate. Koocher and Keith-Spiegel (1998) advise that this process "should be conducted without focusing on whether each option is ethical or feasible and may even include alternatives that might otherwise be considered useless, too risky, too expensive, or inappropriate" (p. 14). Koocher and Keith-Spiegel further point out that occasionally "an option initially considered less attractive may be the best and most feasible choice after all" (p. 14).

In generating possible courses of action, one should also consider the option of taking *no action at all.* In legal decision making, one should always consider the option of deferring a decision or "not doing anything" because such an option can sometimes achieve the desired outcome (R. Nash, personal communication, April 26, 1993). In a problem-solving approach to psychotherapy, there are some problems for which the best solution may involve taking no action at all.

Based on the principle of client autonomy, one should always consider a collaborative approach which includes discussing available options with the client and agreeing on a mutually satisfactory solution (Hill et al., 1995). When an appropriate course of action seems unclear, it may be because there are competing ethical principles which must be identified and prioritized in order to be reconciled. In such situations, consultation with a colleague can be helpful in identifying and prioritizing various conflicting principles. Consultation with a colleague can range from formal supervision to a more informal phone call in which two colleagues discuss various courses of action with respect to possible risks and benefits (B. Alexander, personal communication, April 26, 1993).

Considering Possible Risks and Benefits

The Canadian ethical decision-making model largely incorporates Tymchuk's (1986) approach in its consideration of the likely "short-term, ongoing, long-term consequences" of each course of action on the individuals or groups involved or likely to be affected (p. 40). The most important step in Tymchuk's model involves determining which alternative to implement by looking at the short-term, ongoing, and long-term consequences, and at the likely psychological, social, and economic costs with a risk-benefit analysis of each alternative. In addition to enumerating consequences of each alternative, Koocher and Keith-Spiegel (1998) suggest that the clinician "present any evidence that the various consequences or benefits resulting from each decision will actually occur" (p. 14).

In considering the possible risks and benefits of a course of action, Stadler (1986) has suggested that one apply three simple tests to the selected course of action to ensure that it is appropriate. Incorporating Stadler's tests into their own decision-making model, Herlihy and Corey (1996) offer the following guidelines:

> In applying the test of *justice*, assess your own sense of fairness by determining whether you would treat others the same in this situation. For the test of *publicity*, ask yourself whether you would want your behavior reported in the press. The test of *universality* asks you to assess whether you could recommend the same course of action to another counselor in the same situation. (p. 14)

Universality is typically what distinguishes *ethical* action from *expedient* action (Haas & Malouf, 1995). Ethical actions are based on principles designed to protect the welfare of the client, while expedient actions are based more on factors such as pragmatism and practicality. The concept of universality is expressed by the question, "Would I wish my action to become a universal law?" (Eyde & Quaintance, 1988, p. 149). Haas and Malouf (1995) ask a similar question, "Would I recommend this same course of action to every other person essentially similar to me who is operating in essentially the same circumstances?" (p. 16).

In considering the possible risks and benefits of one's actions, it may be helpful to engage in *consequential* thinking. Eric Harris (personal communication, April 22, 1996) coined the term "projective retrospective" thinking to refer to consequential thinking in which one anticipates the future consequences of one's actions. One is advised to think forward (projectively) and then look back (retrospectively) on one's anticipated actions with respect to their possible consequences (Harris & Remar, 1998). The concept of "projective retrospective" thinking is a recurrent theme in annual risk-management seminars sponsored by the American Psychological Association Insurance Trust (APAIT) (Bennett et al., 1995, 1996, 1997).

Choosing a Course of Action

After considering possible risks and benefits of various alternatives, the next step involves choosing an appropriate course of action. Sinclair et al. (1987) recommend that clinicians consider the questions, "What is the minimal circumstance you can conceive in this situation which would lead you to a different choice of action? What would that action be? Why?" (p. 6). In choosing a course of action, one should consider whether or not the chosen course of action presents any *new* ethical problems. If one anticipates that the chosen course of action might present any new problems, then it may be necessary for the clinician to retrace his or her steps by reviewing applicable standards, considering other alternatives, and obtaining peer consultation.

When encountering a situation in which there is a conflict between ethical standards, Haas and Malouf (1995) recommend that clinicians consider *overarching* ethical principles such as autonomy, responsibility, universality, nonmaleficence, and beneficence. Overarching ethical principles are embodied in the six General Principles of APA (1992) *Ethical Principles*, which refer to rights and responsibilities such as autonomy, self-determination, social responsibility, and concern for others' welfare. For example, in life-threatening emergency situations, there is usually a conflict between the principles of autonomy (letting the client choose) and beneficence (doing good for the client). As Haas and Malouf (1995) point out, "In a conflict between autonomy and beneficence, beneficence is usually given greater weight" (p. 68). On the other hand, particularly in most situations involving competent and reasonable adults, client *autonomy* is usually given considerable weight in the decision-making process. Based on the principle of client autonomy, there should be maximum involvement of the client at every stage of the decision-making process (Hill et al., 1995). Client involvement in a collaborative decision-making process usually increases the likelihood of a positive outcome.

Implementing a Course of Action

While choosing a course of action is based on *principles*, implementing a course of action is often based on *pragmatism*. Implementation of a chosen course of action involves both *practicality* and *prudence*. *Practicality* refers to the likelihood that one can actually implement the course of action, while *prudence* refers to the fact that ethical decisions may at times be costly to the clinician who implements them (Haas & Malouf, 1995). Because ethical actions are based on the concept of universality rather than *expediency*, there are many situations in which an ethical course of action can be time-consuming, demanding, and costly. For example, withholding privileged information in response to a subpoena can be emotionally demanding, time-consuming, and expensive for the clinician (Buchanan, 1997; DeFilippis, Wilbanks, Doverspike, Dsurney, & Bridges, 1997). Implementation of an appropriate course of action often requires personal abilities such as "assertiveness, tenacity, the existence of a supportive social network, and the ability to communicate one's chosen action in noncondescending and humane terms" (Haas & Malouf, 1995, p. 18).

Evaluating the Results of Actions

Most ethical decision-making models conclude with an evaluation of the action taken. If one has engaged in *consequential* thinking prior to choosing a course of action, then it is possible for one's actions to have fairly predictable results. However, good decisions can sometimes lead to bad results. One's best efforts can sometimes result in unintended or even adverse consequences. Evaluating the results of one's actions can lead to modification and improvement of the action plan.

In an article on malpractice prevention, Barnett (1997) concludes, "While psychologists are not required to guarantee positive outcomes, we must make a good faith effort to do so" (p. 22). In an ideal world, a clinician is held accountable not for the *accuracy* of his or her predictions but in the *reasonableness* that has been taken in arriving at such predictions. Ethically responsible behavior is based on the assumption of a reasonable *effort*.

Assuming Responsibility
For Consequences of Actions

Although most ethical decision-making models conclude with an evaluation of the action taken, Eberlein (1987) points out that the Canadian model addresses an important omission of some models. This last step in the decision-making process involves assuming responsibility for the consequences of one's chosen course of action. Assuming responsibility for one's actions may include correcting negative consequences, if any, which may have occurred as the result of one's actions (CPA, 1991). Alternatively, assuming responsibility may also involve continuing the decision-making process if the ethical issue itself has not been resolved satisfactorily. Finally, as Haas and Malouf (1995) point out, "It is also ethically incumbent on the responsible practitioner to learn from his or her mistakes" (p. 19). As a wise colleague once disclosed to me, "Good judgment comes from making mistakes. Great judgment comes from making big mistakes."

UNDERSTANDING LIMITATIONS
OF DECISION-MAKING MODELS

Although ethical problem-solving models can facilitate the decision-making process, such models are not without their limitations. Because decision-making models are based on rationality, there is no way to eliminate the possibility of "self-serving rationalization" (Haas & Malouf, 1995, p. 19). As George Moore (1900) once observed, "The wrong way always seems the more reasonable." The best protection against self-serving rationalization includes consultations with an objective and impartial peer who can see one's *ethical blind spots*. In the absence of peer consultation, there is a *visualization technique* that can be helpful in improving one's objectivity in making good decisions (Doverspike, 1997a, 1999a). Visualize your most respected colleague sitting in the consultation room with you and your patient. While picturing your colleague in front of you, think to yourself, "What would *he* or *she* do? What would *he* or *she* say?" If you're *still* not sure, you should *definitely* consult with a peer.

IDENTIFYING CONFLICTS
BETWEEN ETHICAL AND
LEGAL GUIDELINES

In their discussion of the limitations of ethical decision-making models, Haas and Malouf (1995) raise the question of whether a clinician can make a decision purely on the basis of ethical considerations without regard to legal standards. Their answer is an emphatic *no*. The authors recommend that the clinician first consider the purely ethical or moral aspects of the situation and then consider existing legal standards in terms of the implementation of the decision. On the other hand, Herlihy and Corey (1996) advise that if a legal question exists, legal advice should be obtained first. Because mandatory ethical standards are incorporated into statutory laws in many states, a statutory code or legal reference book may be helpful. In Georgia, for example, a desk reference such as *Law & Mental Health Professional: Georgia* (Remar & Hubert, 1996) may be helpful in identifying applicable legal standards.

In their guidelines for ethical practice, Herlihy and Corey (1996) offer the following four steps for addressing decisions in which there are apparent conflicts between legal, ethical, and institutional forces:

1. *Identify the force that is at issue regarding the counselor's behavior.* Is the principle involved legal, ethical, employer imposed, or demanded by some other force?

2. *If a legal question exists, legal advice should be obtained.* If employed in an agency or institution, counselors should request legal guidance from their immediate supervisor. If in private practice, an attorney should be consulted.

3. *If there is a problem in applying an ethical standard to a particular situation or in understanding the requirements of an ethical standard, the best action a counselor could take is to consult* with colleagues and with those perceived to be experts in the counseling field. Once advice is sought and there seems to be a consensus on the appropriate response in an ethical dilemma, it is essential that the counselor take the advice given (Woody, 1988).

4. *If a force other than law or ethics* (for example, an employer, an accrediting body, or a funding agency) *is suggesting that a counselor take some action he or she perceives to be illegal, the counselor should seek legal advice* to determine whether such action is indeed illegal. If the action seems to be unethical, advice should be sought from colleagues or experts. In the event the counselor determines that an action is illegal or unethical, the counselor should approach the representative of the force in an attempt to resolve the problem in a satisfactory manner. If such an approach is unsuccessful, the counselor should seek legal advice regarding the next course of action. (pp. 288-289)*

SOLVING ETHICAL PROBLEMS
BEFORE THEY ARISE

Although ethical decision-making models offer a *reactive* approach to ethical problem solving, clinicians should consider adopting a *proactive* approach to ethical decision making. Such an approach focuses on *primary prevention* of ethical problems by anticipating and handling potential ethical problems as *technical* problems. A working knowledge of relevant ethical and legal standards allows one to anticipate potential problematic situations before they arise.

Most potential ethical problems can often be minimized or avoided altogether by discussing concerns at the outset. For example, potential misunderstandings related to fee disputes or financial arrangements can be addressed through the use of posted fee schedules and written financial agreements discussed prior to providing services. Potential misunderstandings related to limits of confidentiality can be addressed through the use of ongoing informed consent procedures. Anticipated problems related to issues such as limits of services or premature termination in managed care practice can be addressed in a collaborative manner at the outset of treatment. Potential problems related to dual relationships or boundary violations can be avoided by adopting professional behavior and office policies which demonstrate clear limits and firm boundaries from the first session onward. As a general rule, most potential ethical problems can be avoided through the use of common-sense, respectful attitudes, open communication, and ongoing consultation with colleagues.

SUMMARY OF
DECISION-MAKING GUIDELINES

In summary, ethical decision-making models can provide a framework for putting ethical principles into practice. Such models can be particularly useful in situations in which there are either conflicting or no clear standards. The common features of these models include a sequential decision-making process involving consideration of alternatives, choice of appropriate actions, and evaluation of consequences. When used appropriately, decision-making models can provide some helpful guidelines for achieving an aspirational level of ethical awareness. Although ethical decision-making models offer a reactive approach to ethical problem-solving, clinicians should also consider adopting a proactive approach by using procedures which prevent ethical problems before they arise.

POINTS TO REMEMBER

- Identify the "stake-holders" or parties likely to be affected by the outcome of the situation.

- Identify relevant ethical principles and legal standards of practice.

- Use a "solution-generating" or "brainstorming" process to develop alternative courses of action.

- Consider short-term and long-term risks and benefits of each course of action.

- Choose an appropriate course of action in collaboration with the client.

- Implement the course of action with consideration to practicality and prudence.

- Conduct ongoing evaluation of the results of actions which can lead to modification or improvement of action plan.

- Assume responsibility for consequences of actions. Learn from mistakes.

- Take a proactive approach in preventing ethical problems before they arise.

INFORMED CONSENT ISSUES: PREVENTING ETHICAL PROBLEMS BEFORE THEY ARISE

In an article on avoiding malpractice, Barnett (1997) shares the observation, "Too often I have experienced that sinking feeling in the pit of my stomach when reviewing an ethics complaint, seeing how costly this is to the individuals involved and often how easily it could have been avoided" (p. 20). While ethical decision-making models provide a *reactive* approach to solving ethical problems, the process of informed consent may be viewed as a *proactive* approach to preventing ethical problems before they arise. Informed consent has become an increasingly important concept as clinicians have become more aware of evolving ethical standards and relevant case law. Informed consent has become a popular topic in academic research and in continuing education and risk-management training (Bennett et al., 1995, 1996; Shapiro, 1994; Smith, Graves, Hall, & Paddock, 1994). Although concerns have been raised about whether informed consent procedures provide any protection against legal liability, *failure* to obtain informed consent is a proven area of legal risk (Stromberg & Dellinger, 1993; Weiner & Wettstein, 1993). In an age of increasing litigation, "psychologists can be held liable for failure to obtain appropriate informed consent *even if their subsequent treatment of the patient is exemplary from a clinical perspective*" (Stromberg & Dellinger, 1993, p. 5). In the practice of managed care, informed consent has become a concern as utilization reviewers request confidential information necessary to establish medical necessity, evaluate treatment outcome, and limit services rendered.

At a time when patient satisfaction questionnaires seem to be more popular than psychotherapy outcome studies, informed consent procedures may also make sense from a marketing perspective. An empirical investigation by Sullivan, Martin, and Handelsman (1993) found that a hypothetical male therapist was rated more highly if he used a consent form to promote discussion than an identical therapist who did not use an informed consent procedure. The authors concluded that the use of an informed consent procedure "seems to enhance impressions of trustworthiness and expertness" (p. 162). From an ethical perspective, Handelsman and Galvin (1988) have observed that written consent forms also "have a role in facilitating the ethical goals of informed consent: increasing professionals' self-scrutiny, respecting the autonomy of clients, and allowing clients to enhance their welfare by becoming partners with the therapist in their mental health care" (p. 223).

AN OVERVIEW OF
INFORMED CONSENT

Informed consent can be loosely defined as an agreement which ensures that the patient's participation in treatment is voluntary and based on an understanding of the procedures and their related risks. In the field of medicine, Switankowsky (1998) proposes an autonomy-enhancing model of informed consent in which the patient-physician relationship is viewed as an equal partnership with a common goal of improving the patient's overall health and well-being.

In the field of psychotherapy, Pope and Vasquez (1991) have described informed consent as a dynamic process which involves communication, clarification, and decision making. As the treatment plan changes, so does the ongoing requirement for informed consent. In keeping with the spirit of this dynamic process, Handelsman and Galvin (1988) have developed an outline of questions which can be addressed as part of an informed consent discussion. Designed to facilitate discussion, their outline format includes questions related to outpatient therapy, appointments, confidentiality, and money. In emphasizing the advantages of their question-answer format over narrative forms, Handelsman and Galvin (1988) point out that their question-answer approach may be less overwhelming than a lengthy written form, and the conversational style of their format preserves the patients' right to *refuse* information. Of course, one could argue that a patient's refusal of information could itself later prove problematic. Most proponents (Bennett et al., 1995, 1996; Shapiro, 1994; Younggren, 1995) advocate the use of a signed, detailed, and well-documented informed consent procedure.

UNDERSTANDING THE ETHICAL PRINCIPLES

Ethical issues relevant to informed consent are addressed in APA (1992) *Ethical Standard* 4.02 which in part states, "Psychologists obtain appropriate informed consent to therapy or related procedures, using language that is reasonably understandable to participants" (p. 1605). Although the specific content of informed consent may differ in each situation, there are some basic elements which provide a foundation for understanding the ethical requirements of informed consent. According to APA standards, "Informed consent generally implies that the person (1) has the capacity to consent, (2) has been informed of significant information concerning the procedure, (3) has freely and without undue influence expressed consent, and (4) consent has been appropriately documented" (p. 1605). These four basic components of informed consent overlap with an earlier medico-legal model described in *The Psychologist's Legal Handbook* (Stromberg et al., 1988). Stromberg et al. delineate the four components as "(1) *competency* of the patient, (2) disclosure of *material information*, (3) *understanding* by the patient, and (4) *voluntary consent*" (p. 447). The consent forms contained at the end of this book represent one of several methods for appropriately documenting these basic elements. These consent forms provide significant material information which can be used to facilitate discussion between the psychologist and patient.

DETERMINING CAPACITY TO CONSENT

APA *Ethical Standards* briefly describe four basic elements of informed consent. The first element involves the issue of competence or "capacity to consent," which means that the patient possesses "a basic ability rationally to assess the risks and benefits of treatment" (Stromberg & Dellinger, 1993, p. 5). For informed consent purposes, the issue of competency "means essentially that the person is able to understand the basic purposes and effects (including risks or side effects) of the proposed diagnostic procedure, therapy, or hospitalization" (Stromberg et al., 1988, p. 448). The psychologist has a duty to determine (informally or otherwise) whether the patient is competent to give consent or whether the situation may justify providing some type of service in the absence of fully informed consent. The patient's capacity to consent does not require formal documentation but rather must be based on the psychologist's *understanding* of the person at the time the consent is given (Canter et al., 1994). For informed consent purposes, competency means that "the person is able to understand the basic purposes and effects (including risks or side effects) of the proposed diagnostic procedure, therapy, or hospitalization" (Stromberg et al., 1988, p. 448).

When a patient is legally incapable of giving informed consent, APA *Ethical Standards* require that "psychologists obtain informed permission from a legally authorized person, if such substitute consent is permitted by law" (1992, p. 1605). In addition, the psychologist must inform the patient about the proposed interventions, seek the patient's assent to those interventions, and consider the patient's preferences and best interests. Consultation with a colleague is also advisable in situations in which the patient is unable to give consent (Canter et al., 1994). In cases involving children, APA *Ethical Standards* do not require that the psychologist necessarily obtain the child's agreement, but simply that the psychologist explain the procedures, seek the child's assent, and consider the child's preferences and best interests (Canter et al., 1994). In the case of involuntarily hospitalized inpatients, under almost all state laws, involuntary commitment does not itself imply incompetence (Stromberg & Dellinger, 1993). A more difficult situation arises in situations in which there is some question concerning the patient's capacity to consent. In such cases, the psychologist is advised to engage the patient in discussion, elicit input from others, and document how the patient's rights have been considered and protected (Canter et al., 1994). As Haas and Malouf (1995) advise clinicians, "Assume that the person is competent to give informed consent unless there is clear evidence to the contrary" (p. 68).

PROVIDING SIGNIFICANT
INFORMATION

For a competent person who is fully capable of giving consent, the second basic element of informed consent requires that the person be informed of "significant information" regarding procedures. It is this second element of informed consent that has received the most attention from legal analysts and professional writers (Bennett et al., 1995, 1996; Shapiro, 1994; Stromberg & Dellinger, 1993; Weiner & Wettstein, 1993; Younggren, 1995). Stromberg et al. (1988) point out that courts have focused most closely on the patient's *understanding*, even though it constitutes only one component of competency to give informed consent. The psychologist must provide relevant information and determine whether the person sufficiently *understands* the information necessary to make an informed decision. This provision does not require that any *specific* type of information be provided, but rather that the patient be provided with "significant information." Such information might include issues related to confidentiality, benefits and risks of treatment, and alternative forms of treatment.

Piazza and Baruth (1990) recommend that the psychologist furnish information related to the treatment to be provided, as well as its potential benefits and limitations. Stromberg et al. (1988) state, "The practitioner must disclose all information that a reasonable person would want to consider before deciding to accept or reject treatment, including the nature of treatment, its potential benefits and risks, the existence of any alternative treatments, its benefits and risks, and the benefits and risks of no treatment at all" (p. 449). Haas and Malouf (1995) offer some practical guidelines including, "Put yourself in the patient's place; what information would *you* desire?" (p. 68).

APA *Ethical Standard* 4.01 states, "Psychologists discuss with clients or patients as early as is feasible in the therapeutic relationship appropriate issues, such as the nature and anticipated course of therapy, fees, and confidentiality" (1992, p. 1605). Relevant sections of the *Ethical Standards* include Describing the Nature and Results of Psychological Services, Fees and Financial Arrangements, Structuring the Relationship, Informed Consent to Therapy, Couple and Family Relationships, and Discussing the Limits of Confidentiality. The consent forms contained in the

Appendices of this book address these and other issues related to scope of practice, benefits and risks, alternative procedures, limits of confidentiality, and financial arrangements.

With respect to structuring therapy relationships, APA *Ethical Standard* 4.01 states, "Psychologists make reasonable efforts to answer patients' questions and to avoid misunderstandings about therapy. Whenever possible, psychologists provide oral and/or written information, using language that is reasonably understandable to the patient or client" (1992, p. 1605). The question-answer approach advocated by Handelsman and Galvin (1988) certainly conforms to this standard. Regarding treatment information to be provided, Piazza and Baruth (1990) recommend that the psychologist discuss potential benefits and limitations of treatment. Regarding the issue of confidentiality, while psychologists have traditionally been trained to inform their patients that their communications are confidential, contemporary psychologists are increasingly encouraged to emphasize the *limits* of confidentiality (Bennett et al., 1995, 1996; Shapiro, 1994; Younggren, 1995). For example, some practitioners provide the patient with a list of some of the most common exceptions to confidentiality without assuring the patient that this is a comprehensive list.

Perhaps one of the most comprehensive approaches to informed consent has been outlined by Schlosser and Tower (1991), who require their clients to read and initial each page of a 10-page description of office policies and procedures. Schlosser and Tower (1991) observe, "Prior to using written policies, we would on occasion encounter a difference of opinion regarding expectations, cost, billing procedures, and third-party coverage. Adoption of these materials has reduced such problems significantly" (p. 393).

Regarding financial arrangements, APA *Ethical Standard* 1.25 states, "As early as is feasible in a professional or scientific relationship, the psychologist and patient, client, or other appropriate recipient of psychological services reach an agreement specifying compensation and the billing arrangements" (1992, p. 1602). Such an agreement might include a discussion of fees, payment for missed sessions, billing for phone calls and letters, the use of collection agencies, and financial arrangements should the patient lose their source of income (Handelsman & Galvin, 1988). In the practice of managed care, an informed consent discussion might also include contractual agreements, precertification requirements, limitations in coverage, and termination procedures (Younggren, 1995). Clinicians should provide enough information for the patient to make informed decisions, but not so much information that the patient becomes confused and overwhelmed. As a practical guideline regarding how much significant information to discuss, Haas and Malouf (1995) advise, "If in doubt, inform the person anyway. It is always better to have provided sufficient information than to be accused later of having denied the patient the opportunity to decide for himself or herself" (p. 68).

AVOIDING UNDUE INFLUENCE

The third element of informed consent requires that the patient's consent must be obtained freely and without "undue influence." The psychologist must determine whether the patient has provided consent on an adequately voluntary basis. This would mean that there has been no coercion or undue influence based on the patient's vulnerable condition or other factors (Canter et al., 1994).

Some legal analysts have pointed out that competent and adequately informed consent "will be presumed to be freely given unless there is a *specific indication of fraud, coercion or duress*" (Stromberg et al., 1988, p. 450). Nevertheless, psychologists should remain alert to subtle ways in which undue influence may unwittingly occur, such as emphasizing the benefits while failing to mention the risks of psychotherapy. At the same time, psychologists must decide how "risky" a psychotherapeutic procedure might be before a patient should be informed of the risk in the first place. When discussing such risks with their patients, psychologists must be reasonable and sensitive in presenting the information in a way that does not unduly influence the patient's decision (Andrews, 1984). In some cases, it may be advisable to discuss the limitations rather than the risks of therapy. Stromberg et al. (1988) advise psychologists to inform their therapy patients of "the type of therapy, the approximate length of time treatment may require, the cost of treatment, and any substantial risks or side effects that might reasonably occur as a result of treatment" (p. 449). Because treatment is an ongoing process, the patient must also adequately understand and voluntarily agree to any changes in the ongoing treatment plan.

OBTAINING WRITTEN
DOCUMENTATION

The fourth and final element of informed consent requires that the patient's consent be "appropriately documented." It is important to point out that the APA standard does *not* require a signed consent form. Whether one chooses a more casual question-answer format or a formal, written narrative approach, compliance with APA standards requires that the patient's consent be appropriately documented. Appropriate documentation can range from a signed informed consent form to a brief progress note which records the basic matters discussed (Canter et al., 1994). The recent trend has been more toward the use of a detailed, signed informed consent form (Bennett et al., 1995, 1996; Piazza & Yeager, 1991; Shapiro, 1994; Younggren, 1995). Piazza and Baruth (1990) point out that a signed authorization provides clear evidence that the psychologist and the patient "have discussed the treatment to be provided, its potential benefits, potential limitations, and a statement that the client has given his or her consent to be treated" (p. 315). A flexible approach combining both verbal discussion and written documentation may offer more protection than either method alone. Consistent with Handelsman and Galvin's (1988) question-discussion format, Stromberg et al. (1988) suggest that the psychologist present to the patient a general informed consent form which discloses basic information, with space provided for the psychologist to write in detail or in summary what else was discussed. The form can be signed and initialed by the patient. The combined verbal discussion and written documentation approach "provides persuasive evidence that a conscientious effort to obtain informed consent was made" (Stromberg et al., 1988, p. 451). Stromberg et al. (1988) also describe another option: a two-step process in which a consent form is supplemented by oral discussion, leading to a written statement by the patient designed to demonstrate the patient's understanding of the information. The "written statement" approach has been described as particularly useful because courts have focused most closely on the patient's understanding, even though it constitutes only one component of competency. The consent forms contained in the Appendices of this book represent a formal method for appropriately documenting discussion of the basic elements of informed consent.

EXCEPTIONS TO
INFORMED CONSENT

There are four exceptions to the requirement to obtain informed consent, which are described in *The Psychologist's Legal Handbook* (Stromberg et al., 1988). One exception includes situations in which the patient expressly and specifically waives the right. Such a waiver should be "knowing" or informed. In order to ensure that the waiver is knowing, Stromberg and associates explain that patients should be told that the psychologist "is willing to inform the patient about the treatment, unless the patient would rather that the therapist not inform him, and this should be carefully documented" (p. 452). Stromberg and Dellinger (1993) discuss three other situations in which "informed consent may be reduced or dispensed: (1) in emergencies, either affecting the individual's or the public's health or safety; (2) when the patient lacks the ability to understand or agree, in which case someone else must consent for him; and (3) when disclosure would harm the patient" (pp. 6-7). This last exception, which is also known as "therapeutic privilege," applies when the psychologist intentionally does not inform a patient of certain facts because to do so would harm the patient. Legal precedent for invoking "therapeutic privilege" is based on court decisions which have found that information can be withheld from a patient "when the disclosure poses such a threat of detriment to the patient as to become infeasible or contra-indicated from a medical point of view" (*Canterbury v. Spence,* 1972). However, Stromberg and Dellinger (1993) have noted that most legal writers have cautioned against invoking therapeutic privilege except in "extraordinarily justifiable situations" (p. 6).

An exception to the doctrine of informed consent exists in emergency situations in which there may be a danger to the health or safety of the patient or others. In cases involving emergency situations, "Psychologists should attempt to obtain the best possible version of informed consent in all cases, even when treating distressed patients" (Stromberg et al., 1988, p. 452). One recommendation would be to discuss with each new patient basic reasons for seeking treatment, anticipated costs, treatment effects, and confidentiality issues "*as soon as clinically advisable*" (Stromberg et al., 1988, p. 451). Although APA *Ethical Principles* do not directly address exceptions to informed consent in emergency situations, psychologists are advised to consult with colleagues when dispensing with informed consent in certain research situations. Consultation with a colleague is advisable in situations in which the patient is unable to give consent (Canter et al., 1994). In medical emergency situations, it may also be advisable for the psychologist to obtain input from significant others. Procedural guidelines might include consideration of the patient's best interests, consultation with a peer, obtaining information from next of kin or significant others, and discussion with the patient as soon as clinically advisable. In any event, dispensing with informed consent should be considered the exception rather than the rule.

As discussed earlier, there is an exception to the requirement for obtaining informed consent from legally "incompetent" patients, including minor children. Informed consent procedures for such individuals are addressed by APA *Ethical Standards* which allow "substitute consent" as permitted by law. Substitute consent allows the psychologist to obtain consent from a legally authorized person, such as the parent of a minor child or the guardian of an incompetent person. Even in such situations, however, the child and particularly the older adolescent patient have certain rights to know what is happening. The psychologist has an ethical duty to explain the procedures, seek the child's assent, and consider the child's preferences and best interests.

CONSIDERING LEGAL STANDARDS

Although concerns have been raised about whether informed consent procedures provide any protection against legal liability, *failure* to obtain informed consent is a proven area of legal risk (Stromberg & Dellinger, 1993). Court rulings have shown that practitioners who fail to obtain informed consent may be held liable for a breach of the standard of care (e.g., *Canterbury v. Spence,* 1972; *Clites v. Iowa,* 1980). Stromberg and Dellinger (1993) have pointed out, "Because the patient's informed consent is deemed to have a value in itself, psychologists can be held liable for failure to obtain appropriate informed consent *even if their subsequent treatment of the patient is exemplary from a clinical perspective*" (p. 5). In an age of increasing litigation, psychologists are advised to obtain informed consent which is detailed, discussed, and signed (Bennett et al., 1995, 1996; Piazza & Baruth, 1990; Younggren, 1995). Because such documentation provides a record for the future, most legal analysts recommend the use of a written consent form (Stromberg et al., 1988). Piazza and Baruth (1990) recommend that such authorization be obtained "from every client before or at the time of the first visit" (p. 315). On the other hand, Schlosser and Tower (1991) recommend that their clients take home and review their 10-page office policy form, emphasizing, "Handing out these lengthy materials before a first meeting with a client would likely appear too bureaucratic and impersonal" (p. 393).

As Piazza and Yeager (1991) have observed, "Psychotherapy is increasingly being viewed as a hazardous or invasive procedure, and having a signed statement of informed consent can help reduce the risk of litigation following a negative treatment experience" (p. 344). The use of a written consent form is especially important "if consent is given on behalf of another (such as a minor child) or is a consent for innovative, confrontational, or risky therapies" (Stromberg et al., 1988, p. 447). On a related matter, it is interesting to note that the *American Psychological Association Insurance Trust Liability Policy* requires that psychologists who offer services "involving physical contact" with patients submit a copy of their "release form" with their insurance renewal application (APAIT, 1996, p. 2). As a general rule, the more invasive or innovative the procedure, the greater the need for adequately informed consent and careful documentation of procedures.

CONSIDERING MANAGED CARE

The practice of managed care raises some complex informed consent issues. Several of these issues have been summarized by Younggren (1995) who has noted that insured patients who actually understand their benefits packages are usually the exception rather than the rule. Patients who think they have unlimited insurance benefits are typically unaware that their maximum benefits are rarely authorized by their managed care company reviewers. For this reason, when discussing financial arrangements with the patient, it may be helpful to explain differences between health insurance and managed care so that the patient can better appreciate how their particular plan operates (Doverspike, 1995). While insurance verification and managed care precertification have become standard operating procedures for most psychologists, Younggren (1995) points out that most patients do not understand that their psychologist may have to obtain prior authorization for therapy and related procedures. In cases involving diagnostic assessment, procedures such as psychological testing typically require prior authorization and they sometimes require submission of the written report to the managed care company. Most patients are surprised to learn that their managed care company will have access to confidential information including telephonic reviews, progress reports, and even therapy notes. There are occasions when it may be advisable to have the patient present during telephone precertification or utilization reviews (Doverspike, 1995). Having the patient present during such calls can improve communication, encourage a collaborative atmosphere, and provide the patient with a better understanding of the review process.

Given the managed care treatment philosophy of short-term crisis intervention, psychologists are obliged to discuss at the outset of therapy issues related to termination and limitations of services (Younggren, 1995). Regarding limitations to services that can be anticipated because of limitations in financing, APA *Ethical Standard* 1.25 requires that this be discussed with the patient or other appropriate recipient of services "as early as is feasible" (1992, pp. 1602-1603). Regarding interruption of services, APA *Ethical Standard* 4.08 requires that psychologists provide for appropriate resolution of responsibility of patient care "in the event that the employment or contractual relationship ends, with paramount consideration given to the welfare of the patient or client" (1992, p. 1606). Given the preference of many managed care patients to continue receiving services beyond those authorized as "medically necessary" by their case managers, it is important to manage the patient's expectations from the outset. When structuring the therapy relationship and anticipating a limit in the number of sessions authorized or financed by a managed care company, the prudent practitioner discusses options in advance. These options may include consideration of time-limited sessions, termination when initial goals are achieved, referral to a public mental health center, as well as the option of patient self-payment. Most managed care contracts permit the patient to self-pay for services which are not considered medically necessary *if* such an arrangement is clarified and agreed upon in advance. Appendix F (pp. 77-78) of this book contains a consent form which can be used to document the patient's understanding of unauthorized services beyond medical necessity.

USING INFORMED
CONSENT FORMS

The consent forms contained in the Appendices were designed specifically for my hospital practice which includes diagnostic consultations, psychological assessment, neuropsychological testing, and brief psychotherapy. To the extent that such services do not always involve therapy, one could argue that it is not necessary to obtain informed consent. On the other hand, since one could argue that "related procedures" include psychological assessment and consultation, the most prudent course of action would be to discuss these procedures and obtain the patient's informed consent. Documentation of informed consent for evaluations is particularly important in the case of forensic testimony, child custody evaluations, and independent consultative examinations, because such evaluations are often associated with litigation and professional liability complaints. Appendix D on pages 73-74 of this book contains a consent form which can be used to document informed consent for independent consultative evaluations.

Because informed consent is an ongoing, dynamic, and continuing process of informing the patient about what may be required, the written consent forms should never be a substitute for ongoing discussion with the patient. Merely having a patient "sign off" on several forms at intake is not sufficient to have properly established informed consent. Written consent forms should always be accompanied by a discussion of the issues to ensure the patient's understanding (Handelsman & Galvin, 1988; Schlosser & Tower, 1991).

With regard to the development of an appropriate consent form, it should be emphasized that the consent forms contained in the Appendices do not represent static documents but rather each form represents one frame in an ongoing process of development.

Beginning with a prototype consent form developed several years ago, the consent forms have undergone literally dozens of revisions based on legal advice, peer consultation, revised ethical principles, and evolving standards of practice. Each paragraph reflects a situation and each sentence addresses a question that has arisen in my own clinical practice. A useful consent form provides a balance between general and specific information. As Handelsman and Galvin (1988) observe, "It is hard to avoid some information that is so specific that it does not apply to many clients or so general that it conveys almost nothing" (p. 224).

Although these forms specify "psychologist" as the provider and cite relevant sections of the American Psychological Association's *Ethic's Code*, they can be easily modified for other professions. Depending on the provider's preferences, terms such as "client" may also be substituted for "patient" and the descriptions of services may be modified to fit your practice.

Because diagnostic and assessment services are often requested by a third party such as a referring physician, the consent forms place an emphasis on standards related to limits of confidentiality and release of information. These forms provide basic significant information which can be discussed with the patient to ensure the patient's understanding. In cases where certain information should be emphasized to the patient, the psychologist may choose to underline the material and have the patient place his or her initials next to such sections. In cases where the patient may object to certain conditions, the psychologist has the option of striking through a section which can be initialed by the psychologist and patient. In cases where the patient raises several objections or refuses to sign the form, the psychologist should consider the implications of the patient's actions in deciding whether to provide services under such circumstances.

Because these forms were designed specifically for an assessment-oriented practice, they do not address all of the issues which may arise as part of an ongoing informed consent discussion in other types of practices. The forms can be modified and customized as needed for other specialty practices and procedures. Some practitioners may prefer the use of a generic form which can be tailored for each patient by filling in specific information, while others may prefer to use a series of separate forms or brochures that address relevant issues as they arise. Other areas of informed consent discussion might include basic issues such as cancellation policies, emergency and weekend coverage, and the use of telephone consultations. In the practice of managed care, issues related to the release of specific information may require ongoing discussion and documentation of informed consent. More detailed informed consent procedures might be required for more complex clinical situations such as child custody evaluations, independent consultative examinations, biofeedback treatment, or the use of hypnosis or other specialized treatment procedures. Therapists working in more controversial areas such as "recovered memories" would be well advised to consult with their attorneys regarding appropriate informed consent procedures.

Sample consent forms are contained in the Appendices of this book.* Appendix A (pp. 61-64) contains an informed consent for psychological services form which addresses clinical services related to scope of practice, assumption of risks and benefits, limits of confidentiality, and release of information. Appendix B (pp. 65-68) contains a disclosure form regarding informed consent for financial responsibility, which addresses issues related to fees for services, insurance filing, managed care contracts, guarantee of payment, billing and collections, and release of information for third-party payments. For clinicians choosing a more informal approach to informed consent considerations, Appendix C (pp. 69-71) provides an informed consent checklist which includes topics which may be discussed and appropriately documented during the course of an interview. Appendix D (pp. 73-74) includes a form for documenting informed consent for third-party-requested, independent consultative examinations. Appendix E (pp. 75-76) contains a letter of agreement regarding financial responsibility for expert testimony. Appendix F (pp. 77-78) illustrates a statement of understanding for managed care patients requesting services which are either unauthorized or which do not meet medical necessity criteria. Appendix G (pp. 79-80) illustrates the importance of documenting a record of conversations with managed care case managers or others concerned with the patient's treatment.

---

*These consent forms and the contents of this book are not intended to provide legal advice and the information contained in it should not be relied upon for legal advice. The reader is encouraged to contact a qualified attorney for legal advice regarding state laws governing informed consent.

SUMMARY OF INFORMED
CONSENT CONSIDERATIONS

To use an old proverb, "An ounce of prevention is worth a pound of cure." From a risk-management perspective, informed consent procedures help prevent ethical problems before they arise. Written consent forms provide a means of documenting informed consent, but such forms should never be used as a substitute for sound legal advice and a working knowledge of ethical principles. When used appropriately, written consent forms can provide some helpful guidelines for facilitating open communication, ongoing discussion, clarification of choices, and decision making.

POINTS TO REMEMBER

- Determine the client's capacity to give consent.

- Assume the client is competent unless there is evidence to the contrary.

- Provide enough significant information for the client to make a decision.

- Manage client expectations from the outset of therapy.

- Avoid undue influence in the client's decision-making process.

- Obtain written documentation of informed decisions.

RESPONDING ETHICALLY TO COMPLAINTS AND INVESTIGATIONS

Sooner or later, anyone may be faced with a situation in which one's best efforts must be explained in light of a complaint or investigation by a third party. In such situations, the best strategy is to have already followed some of the ideas which have been outlined in the previous sections.

RESPONDING TO THE NOTICE OF INVESTIGATION

Known in one state as the "Notice to Complainee of Investigation" (GPA, 1996, p. 11), some variation of the form letter on page 50 is often a psychologist's first notice that an ethics complaint has been filed by a former client. Acknowledging the certified letter as an "unpleasant experience" is an understatement. An appropriate description of the experience would probably include a mixture of words and feelings such as anger and fear, panic and paranoia, or frustration and embarrassment. At a recent public gathering of psychologists, one colleague described the experience as being like a combination of a panic disorder and posttraumatic stress disorder. Amidst the flood of emotions which accompany this type of experience, there are some useful reminders which may be helpful to colleagues undergoing an ethics investigation.

Dear Dr. [Professional's Name]:

On [Date] your State Association Ethics Committee received a complaint against you from [Complainant]. The complaint has been assigned to one of the Committee's investigative panels. The panel is charged with determining whether sufficient cause exists for the complaint to be formally docketed with the Committee.

Enclosed please find a copy of the completed Ethics Complaint Form and all materials submitted by [Complainant], a copy of the *Ethical Principles* which [Complainant] claims are at issue, and a copy of the Committee's Rules and Procedures.

Please file a response within 45 days of receipt of this letter. If you need additional time, the panel will consider extending the time to respond for good cause if a written request to extend the time is made within 45 days of receipt of this letter.

We request that you respond to the complaint personally and in writing. Please be as complete as possible. You are, of course, free to consult with legal counsel but your response should be from you and not from a third party acting on your behalf. You are responsible for any legal expenses incurred. Please understand that all information submitted by you shall become a part of the record in this matter and could be used if any further proceedings ensue.

We recognize that receiving a complaint is stressful and unpleasant even if the complaint is without merit. If you have any questions or concerns, please do not hesitate to contact the undersigned directly.

Sincerely yours,

[Committee Member]

THERE IS NO SUCH THING AS A FRIVOLOUS COMPLAINT

A good starting point is to remember that there is no such thing as a frivolous complaint. Given the amount of time and the enormous emotional (and often financial) resources required to resolve formal complaints, it is important to take all client dissatisfactions seriously. A good working relationship may help guarantee that your client will report dissatisfactions directly to *you* rather than to someone else. In the event that your client does make a complaint directly to you, the best course of action would be to take the complaint seriously, discuss the client's concerns, obtain consultation with a peer, work toward a satisfactory resolution, and document your actions in writing (Doverspike, 1997a, 1999a). In the event that your client makes a complaint to someone else, including filing a complaint with an ethics committee, keep reading.

BEING A COLLEAGUE, NOT AN ADVERSARY

Before responding to the "Notice to Complainee of Investigation," it may be helpful to remember that ethics committee members are your colleagues, not your adversaries. They are simply colleagues who have an interest in ethics education, who usually view their role as educative in nature, and who have been asked to volunteer their time by reviewing cases. There is probably nothing that an ethics committee member likes better than to review a well-documented record which indicates that the psychologist in question provided a high standard of care. On the other hand, there is probably nothing that an ethics committee member dislikes worse than to review a colleague's response of self-righteous indignation. Colleagues who are unjustly accused of wrongdoing are usually capable of rising to the occasion in a mutually respectful and collegial manner.

BEING A BEHAVIORIST WHEN EXPLAINING DETAILS

In formulating your response to a complaint letter, remember that your colleagues on the committee will not know anything about how you handled a case except for the information provided by you and your client. Because your client has already filed a complaint, which is unlikely to portray your view of the situation, your main task is to explain your side of the story. Remember that your peer reviewers will not know your side of the story unless your provide the details. Regardless of your theoretical perspective, think like a behaviorist and explain what happened in terms of specific details, behaviors, and events. It is important to focus on the details "with scrupulous attention" (Crawford, 1994, p. 92). If you kept good case notes, your record will be valuable in helping you recall specific details. If you did not keep good notes, remember the advice, "When in doubt, tell the truth."

BEING ABLE TO EXPLAIN
WHAT YOU DID AND
WHY YOU DID IT

To use the rationale of Stromberg et al. (1988), explain what you did and why you did it, as well as what you didn't do and why you didn't do it. When making clinical and ethical decisions in difficult situations, a good clinical record should reflect a careful decision-making process. On an aspirational level, an ideal record would show (a) what your choice was expected to accomplish, (b) why you believed it would be effective, (c) any risks that might have been involved and why they were justified, (d) what alternative treatments were considered, (e) why they were rejected, and (f) what steps were taken to improve the effectiveness of your decision or chosen treatment (Soisson et al., 1987). When applying these guidelines to an ethics complaint investigation, remember that an ideal response should show a careful decision-making process or a coherent rationale for your actions.

LEARNING NOT TO
BLAME THE CLIENT

Individuals with severe characterological disturbance, particularly those with paranoid or borderline personality disorders, may be more likely to file complaints (Bennett et al., 1995, 1996, 1997; Harris & Remar, 1998). However, don't think of the patient's pathology as a defense of your behavior. Although you may feel like it, blaming the patient is not a good response to an ethics complaint investigation. Because ethical decisions are based on *principles*, explain your actions and decisions in terms of *principles* and not *personalities*.

LEARNING HOW TO
TURN ERRORS INTO AMENDS

In moral theory, restitution of an injury caused by a past transgression can be achieved by recognizing the injury, acknowledging one's wrongdoing, and making amends by taking steps to correct the past action and modify present actions.

In ethical practice, the overarching ethical principle of *nonmaleficence* is concerned with avoiding harm to others. *Ethical Standard* 1.14 states, "Psychologists take reasonable steps to avoid harming their patients or clients, research participants, students, and others with whom they work, and to minimize harm where it is foreseeable and unavoidable" (APA, 1992, p. 1601).

Mistakes happen. Because correcting a mistake may sometimes ameliorate a situation in which a complaint has been filed, be sure to explain any actions that were taken to avoid or minimize harm to the client or others. From a risk-management perspective, there are occasions in which correcting a mistake can sometimes turn a potentially negative situation into a positive one.

SHOWING CONCERN FOR
YOUR CLIENT'S WELFARE

Just as a good patient record is one that shows that you are a careful and conscientious clinician, a good peer review response is one that shows you are a caring and concerned practitioner. When reviewing your written response to an ethics complaint investigation, your peers on the committee may read between the lines for indications that your actions and decisions demonstrated appropriate concern for the welfare of your client and others. Gutheil (1980) recommends that one's notes reflect active concern for the patient's welfare.

BEING ABLE TO NOTE
ANY PEER CONSULTATIONS

Sooner or later, everyone faces a situation in which one's best efforts can result in adverse consequences. In such situations, one of the best defenses for one's actions is to have already obtained and documented consultation with a colleague (Doverspike, 1997a, 1999a). Peer consultation means talking with a respected colleague who is impartial, objective, and knowledgeable. Documentation of such consultation will at least demonstrate careful consideration of appropriate standards of care. If your actions or decisions in a case were guided in part by consultation with a colleague, be sure to mention such consultation in your response.

THINKING IN TERMS OF
ASPIRATIONAL BEHAVIOR

Aspirational obligations represent ideals or the ethical "ceiling" of behavior while mandatory requirements represent minimal standards or the "floor" of ethical behavior (Haas & Malouf, 1995, p. 4). Aspirational ethical obligations represent the ideal achievement of excellence embodied in the six general statements contained in the APA *Ethical Principles of Psychologists*, while *mandatory* requirements represent the enforceable ethical standards delineated in the more specific *Ethical Standards* or *Code of Conduct*. When responding to an ethics investigation, think how your actions and decisions should reflect an *aspirational* level of behavior.

BEING AWARE OF
PROCEDURES AND DEADLINES

Remember that it is important to comply with procedural deadlines. In most cases, one's first notification of a complaint may come in the form of a certified letter explaining the complaint and requesting a written response within a specified time period. A careful and conscientious psychologist responds within the time period, or requests an extension of time before the deadline has passed. A psychologist who responds a week or two beyond the deadline may give the impression that one is not concerned with such details. If you cannot meet a deadline requirement, it is better to ask for an extension *before* rather than *after* the deadline has passed.

UNDERSTANDING THE
COMMITTEE FINDINGS

Known in one state as a "Committee Finding of No Violation" (GPA, 1996), some version of the following form letter is often the psychologist's last formal notice that an ethics investigation has been closed. With the exception of dismissing a complaint before an investigation even begins, this letter usually represents the most favorable outcome of a complaint that has been successfully resolved and closed:

Dear Dr. [Professional's Name]:

Your State Professional Association Ethics Committee has reviewed the formal charges filed against you by [Complainant]. The Committee finds that there has been no violation of the *Ethical Principles* and has dismissed the complaint. This concludes the proceedings before the Committee.

Sincerely yours,

[Committee Member]

TURNING A NEGATIVE
INTO A POSITIVE

The final stage of an ethics complaint resolution should involve making some sense of it all. In the words of Aldous Huxley (1956), "Experience is not what happens to you, it is what you *do* with what happens to you."

Regardless of the result of an investigation, cynicism does not have to be a final outcome. Following the resolution and closure of the investigation, the next step is to take the "unpleasant experience" and learn from it, gain insight into yourself, and grow in your understanding of others. One's ultimate goal in this regard would be to make some *meaning* of what has happened, and transform the circumstances into something positive.

SUMMARY OF RESPONDING
TO ETHICS COMPLAINTS

Mistakes happen. Good motives can lead to bad results. A clinician may be faced with a situation in which one's actions must be explained in response to a formal complaint. Given the amount of resources which are required to resolve complaints, it is important to take all client dissatisfactions seriously. When client dissatisfactions do arise to the level of a formal complaint, it is important to explain what happened in terms of specific details, behaviors, and events. An ideal response should show a careful decision-making process or a coherent rationale for one's actions. Regardless of the outcome of an ethics complaint, the unpleasant experience of an investigation can be beneficial if one can gain insight, grow in understanding others, and transform the circumstances into something positive.

POINTS TO REMEMBER

- Remember there is no such thing as a frivolous complaint.

- Be a colleague, not an adversary.

- Be a good behaviorist when explaining details.

- Be able to explain what you did and why you did it.

- Learn not to blame the client.

- Learn how to turn errors into amends.

- Show concern for your client's welfare.

- Be able to note any peer consultations.

- Think in terms of aspirational behavior.

Continued ➡

- Be aware of procedures and deadlines.

- Understand the committee findings.

- Turn negative experiences into positive ones.

APPENDICES

<u>**APPENDIX A**</u>

INFORMED CONSENT FOR
PSYCHOLOGICAL SERVICES

I hereby voluntarily apply for and consent to psychological services provided by the undersigned psychologist. This consent applies to myself, child, ward, or patient named below. Since I have the right to refuse services at any time, I understand and agree that my continued participation implies voluntary informed consent.

Limitations of Services. I understand that psychological services are limited to psychological evaluation, assessment, consultation, and intervention. I understand that evaluation and assessment services may also include the use of psychological and neuropsychological tests. I understand that intervention services may include counseling and brief psychotherapy. I understand that the undersigned psychologist is not warranting a cure or offering any guarantee of results or improvement of any condition.

Assumption of Risks. I understand that the potential benefits of undergoing psychological services may include obtaining a professional opinion and an increased understanding of myself. I understand that potential risks may include limited predictive validity of psychological assessment procedures, possible disagreement with the opinions offered to me, and possible emotional distress concerning my situation. I understand that alternative procedures include services provided by another psychologist, psychiatrist, or mental health professional.

Limits of Confidentiality. I understand and agree that my disclosures and communications are considered privileged and confidential, except to the extent that I authorize a release of information, or under certain other conditions listed below. I understand that confidential and privileged information may be released without my consent or authorization in the following circumstances recognized by American Psychological Association Guidelines (1987, p. 12): (1) where abuse or harmful neglect of children, the elderly, or disabled or incompetent individuals is known or reasonably suspected; (2) where the validity of a will of a former patient is contested (although this condition may not apply in some states); (3) where such information is necessary for the psychologist to defend against a malpractice action brought by the patient; (4) where an immediate threat of physical violence against a readily identifiable victim is disclosed to the psychologist; (5) in the context of civil commitment proceedings, where an immediate threat of self-inflicted damage is disclosed to the psychologist; or (6) where the patient or client, by alleging mental or emotional damages in litigation, puts his or her mental state at issue (although this condition may not apply in some states); and (7) where the patient [or client] is examined pursuant to a court order. I hold the undersigned psychologist harmless for releasing information under any of the above conditions.

Release of Information. I understand that my records may be protected under federal regulations governing Confidentiality of Alcohol and Drug Abuse Patient Records, and cannot be disclosed without my written consent unless otherwise provided for in the regulations. By authorizing a release of information, I understand that I am waiving the confidential nature of the patient-psychologist relationship. I authorize the release of information as necessary for the purpose of the undersigned psychologist obtaining consultation regarding my evaluation or treatment. If I am a hospitalized inpatient, I understand and agree that the undersigned psychologist may discuss my evaluation and treatment with my physician, hospital staff, utilization review staff, and others concerned with my care. I authorize the release of any and all information requested by my managed care company or insurance carrier for the purpose of processing my insurance claim and obtaining payment for services. If I am entitled to Medicare or managed care benefits, I authorize the release of information to Medicare or to my managed care company. By authorizing the release of information to an insurance company or other third party, I understand that the information may become part of the third party's records and that the undersigned psychologist can no longer control any subsequent release of that information. The undersigned psychologist has informed me that should I ever authorize a general release of my medical records to or from an insurance company or other third party, it is possible that the third party's copy of my psychological records could possibly be released by the third party without the undersigned psychologist's knowledge. I understand that the undersigned psychologist cannot prevent any hospital, physician's office, insurance company, or others from releasing or redisclosing information to the Medical Information Bureau (MIB, Inc.) or other agencies or persons. I hold the undersigned psychologist harmless for any secondary release or redisclosure of my report made by the hospital, physician's office, insurance company, medical information bureau, or any person or agency to whom the report is originally released. After giving consideration to the extent of this release, I specifically direct and authorize the undersigned psychologist to exchange confidential information and discuss his or her opinions with the following agencies or persons named below for the purpose of providing information about my evaluation or treatment:

_____

_____

_____

(Individuals or organizations to whom information may be released)

Statement of Understanding. I understand that I may revoke this consent at any time except to the extent that action has been taken in reliance on it, and that in any event this consent will expire automatically as follows: I understand that my consent for release of information will be considered valid for twelve (12) months following the date below. I acknowledge that I voluntarily consent to the above conditions and that this consent form is valid during any related claims. I certify that I have read this form or that it has been read and explained to me in terms which I understand. My questions have been answered to my satisfaction, all blank spaces on the form have been completed, and all statements of which I do not approve have been stricken. By signing this form, I understand and agree with the terms and conditions of this form.

_____   _____

PATIENT'S SIGNATURE   DATE

_____   _____

PSYCHOLOGIST'S SIGNATURE   DATE

APPENDIX B

INFORMED CONSENT FOR FINANCIAL RESPONSIBILITY

Financial Responsibility. I understand and agree that I will be charged a fee for all direct and indirect professional services rendered on my behalf. The undersigned psychologist charges a fee of $_____ per hour for clinical services; $_____ per hour for expert testimony, office depositions, and review or preparation of documents; and $_____ per hour for expert testimony in civil procedures and courtroom appearances. Fees for standard *Current Procedural Terminology* (CPT; American Medical Association, 1997) codes include $_____ per hour for initial diagnostic interview (90801); $_____ per 45-50 minutes for individual psychotherapy interview (90806); $_____ per 75-80 minutes for extended individual psychotherapy interview (90808); and $_____ per hour for psychological testing, scoring, interpretation, and preparation of report (96100). I understand that the undersigned psychologist may charge his or her hourly fee on a prorated basis for other procedures. Billable services may include (but are not limited to) any or all of the following direct (face-to-face) services: conducting clinical interview; making behavioral observations; or administering psychological tests. Billable services may also include (but are not limited to) any or all of the following indirect services: reviewing hospital chart or medical records; obtaining history and background information; providing staff consultation; and the administration, scoring, and interpretation of psychometric and projective tests. Preparation of a written report is estimated at a minimum of two (2) hours. There is a minimum charge of one-fourth (¼) hour for any indirect service rendered on my behalf, including any phone calls conducted for the purpose of obtaining background information or releasing information. There is a

$_____ charge for records retrieval, photocopying, and mailing of any subsequent reports or records after the initial reports have been released to those authorized to receive them by this consent form. I understand and agree that some tests may be charged on a per-test (rather than hourly) basis which includes both direct and indirect services such as administration, scoring, and interpretation. I understand and agree that testing time and charges may include scoring and analysis of data with preparation of a written report, which requires more time than the face-to-face direct time that the undersigned psychologist spends with the patient.   Estimated charges for psychological consultation (including interview, ad-ministration and scoring of tests, and preparation of report) may range between $_____ and $_____.

Billing and Collections. I understand and agree that professional services are rendered and charged to me and not to an insurance company. In consideration of the services rendered, I promise to pay the undersigned psychologist all of his or her charges and to make payment in full upon receipt of such billing, which may be sent to the address listed in my records.   In the event that the undersigned patient is entitled to benefits of any type arising out of any insurance policy, I hereby assign any insurance benefits to the undersigned psychologist.   I understand and agree that the undersigned psychologist may not know specific information about my specific insurance policy and that he or she is not responsible for actions taken by my insurance company.   I understand and agree that I will be responsible for payment of any charges or services which are not covered by my insurance company. In the case of Medicare claims for which payment is denied and for which I have received advance written notice and determination that medical necessity for services is not justified, I agree in ad-vance to pay the undersigned psychologist all of his or her charges and to make payment in full upon receipt of such billing.   Al-though I may settle my account directly with the undersigned psychologist, I authorize that he or she may use a professional billing company to file paper or electronic insurance claims and bill me for any unpaid balance on my account. I understand and agree that the undersigned psychologist may refer accounts past due ninety (90) days to a collection agency or attorney of his or her choice, with information released as necessary for collection purposes. I specifically authorize the undersigned psychologist to release information to a billing company, collection agency, and/or attorney as necessary for billing and collection purposes. I understand that if I do not settle my account within ninety (90) days, and if my account is assigned to an attorney or collection agency, this may adversely affect my credit. I hold the undersigned psychologist harmless for any adverse consequences which may derive from his or her assignment of my account to a collection agency or attorney.

Release of Information. I specifically authorize the release of any and all information, including diagnosis, procedure codes, itemized list of tests, and psychological report, requested by my insurance or managed care company for the purpose of obtaining prior authorization of services, processing my claim, or considering payment for services. I understand and agree that the undersigned psychologist may communicate by phone and in writing with my insurance or managed care company for the purpose of conducting utilization reviews and providing treatment reports. I understand and agree that utilization reviews and treatment reports may require the written or telephonic release of confidential information such as progress notes, progress reports, and psychological reports. I also authorize the undersigned psychologist to release any information concerning preexisting conditions or previous treatment. I specifically direct and authorize the undersigned psychologist to exchange information, including release of a psychological report and progress notes, and discuss his or her opinions with the following agencies or persons named below, for the purpose of authorizing services, conducting utilization reviews, providing treatment reports, obtaining payment, and balance billing:

_____

_____

_____

(Individuals or organizations to whom information may be released)

Managed Care Contracts. I understand that the undersigned psychologist has contracts with several managed care companies and preferred provider organizations, in which case the terms of those contracts may rule over those of this consent form. In the event that any of the terms of this consent form might conflict with any of the undersigned psychologist's contracts with managed care companies or preferred provider organizations, the terms of those managed care contracts will control.

Statement of Understanding. I understand that I may revoke the consent for release of information at any time except to the extent that action has been taken in reliance on it, and that in any event this consent expires automatically as follows: I understand that my consent for release of information will be considered valid for thirty (30) days after the date my account is paid in full, or for twelve (12) months following the date below, whichever date is later. I acknowledge that I voluntarily consent to the above conditions and that this authorization form is valid during any related claims. I certify that I have read this form or that it has been read and explained to me in terms which I have understood. My questions have been answered to my satisfaction, all blank spaces on the form have been completed, and all statements of which I do not approve have been stricken. By signing this form, I understand and agree with the terms and conditions of this form.

_____   _____

PATIENT'S SIGNATURE   DATE

_____   _____

PSYCHOLOGIST'S SIGNATURE   DATE

APPENDIX C

INFORMED CONSENT CHECKLIST

Information To Be
Provided As Early As Feasible

✔ Provider's education, credentials, and specialty training

✔ Provider's philosophy and scope of practice

✔ Provider's training and experience with particular disorders

✔ Provider's policies and procedures:

  ▷ Fees for direct services (assessment, psychological testing, psychotherapy)
  ▷ Fees for indirect services (telephone calls, report writing, letters)
  ▷ Financial arrangements and third-party payments
  ▷ Limits of insurance or managed care coverage
  ▷ Estimated length of treatment and sessions

✔ Discussion of possible benefits of treatment:

  ▷ Improved functioning in social and family settings
  ▷ Improved work performance
  ▷ Decrease of presenting symptoms and problems
  ▷ Improved ability to solve problems
  ▷ Improved ability to achieve goals

✔ Discussion of possible risks of treatment:

    ▷ Social stigma, shame, or personal embarrassment

    ▷ Stirring up of unpleasant memories

    ▷ Implications of later insurability and employment

✔ Discussion of alternatives and adjuncts to treatment:

    ▷ Risks of allowing the condition to remain untreated

    ▷ Consideration of medication consultation

✔ Discussion of privacy, privilege, and confidentiality:

    ▷ Discussion of limits of confidentiality

    ▷ Authorized releases of information

    ▷ Mandatory reporting requirements

    ▷ Subpoenas and court orders

    ▷ Duty-to-protect issues

Information To Be
<u>Provided As Ongoing Discussion</u>

✔ Provider's intervention techniques:

    ▷ Discussion of provider's approach to treatment

    ▷ Homework assignments

    ▷ Conjoint sessions, group therapy, or family sessions

    ▷ The use of psychological assessment instruments

    ▷ Audio and video recordings of sessions

✔ Discussion of privacy, privilege, and confidentiality:

    ▷ Ongoing discussion of limits of confidentiality

    ▷ Third-party requests for information

✔ Consideration of alternatives and adjuncts to treatment:

    ▷ Consideration of medication consultation
    ▷ Risks of premature termination of treatment

Information To Be Provided
Under Special Circumstances

✔ Discussion of emergency procedures:

    ▷ Coverage of back-up or on-call services
    ▷ Policies regarding after-hours or "crisis" calls
    ▷ Policies regarding hospitalization

✔ Discussion of privacy, privilege, and confidentiality:

    ▷ Mandated reporting requirements
    ▷ Subpoenas and court orders

✔ Discussion of high-risk situations:

    ▷ Recovered memories considerations
    ▷ Duty-to-protect situations
    ▷ Legal proceedings and litigation

✔ Discussion of innovative, risky, or unusual techniques:

    ▷ Nonstandardized assessment procedures
    ▷ Psychotherapy techniques not empirically validated
    ▷ Invasive therapeutic techniques

APPENDIX D

INFORMED CONSENT FOR INDEPENDENT CONSULTATIVE EXAMINATION

I understand and agree that I am undergoing an Independent Consultative Examination by the undersigned psychologist at the request of the interested third party listed below. I understand that the undersigned psychologist will prepare a written report which will include (but may not be limited to) a reason for referral, background information, social history, alcohol and drug history (if applicable), behavioral observations, test results, clinical interpretations, diagnostic classification, and summary and recommendations.

Release of Information. I specifically direct and authorize the undersigned psychologist to exchange information, release a written psychological report, and/or discuss his or her opinions with the interested third-party agency, institution, and/or persons named below. I understand and agree that the undersigned psychologist's report and opinions, including all results and findings from my psychological testing and examination, will be released to the third party listed below. I also hold the undersigned psychologist harmless for any secondary release or redisclosure of my report made by the interested third-party agency, institution, and/or persons named below to whom the report is originally authorized for release.

Explanation of Assessment Results. American Psychological Association (APA; 1992) *Ethical Standard* 2.09 requires that psychologists provide an explanation of assessment results unless the nature of the relationship is clearly explained in advance to the person being assessed, and precludes provision of the assessment results (such as in some organizational consulting, preemployment or security screening, and forensic evaluations). Consistent with APA *Ethical Standard* 2.09, I understand and agree in advance that the nature of the relationship precludes the provision of an explanation of assessment results to myself. In other words, I understand and agree that I will NOT have access to the results, findings, and opinions of the undersigned psychologist's evaluation. I understand and agree that the results and findings of this examination will become the property of the third party listed below. Should I ever request the results or findings of this examination from the undersigned psychologist, I understand that he or she will not release the information to me but that he or she will provide me with a copy of this agreement and forward any written requests to the third party listed below.

Voluntary Informed Consent. I acknowledge that I voluntarily consent to the above conditions and that this authorization form is valid during all related claims. I certify that I have read this form or that it has been read and explained to me in terms which I understand. My questions have been answered to my satisfaction and any blank spaces on the form have been completed. By signing this form, I understand and agree with the terms and conditions of this form.

_____   _____
THIRD PARTY'S SIGNATURE   DATE

_____   _____
PATIENT'S SIGNATURE   DATE

_____   _____
PSYCHOLOGIST'S SIGNATURE   DATE

APPENDIX E

LETTER OF AGREEMENT REGARDING FINANCIAL RESPONSIBILITY FOR EXPERT TESTIMONY

I understand that I, _____, have requested an expert testimony and opinion from the undersigned psychologist. I understand that by providing expert testimony by legal deposition or courtroom appearance, the undersigned psychologist will be rendering a service to myself and my client.

I understand that I will be charged a fee for all direct and indirect professional services rendered on behalf of myself or my client. The undersigned psychologist will charge a fee of $____ per hour for review of files and documents, telephone conferences, travel and waiting time, expert testimony, office depositions, and review or preparation of documents relating to the deposition. There will be a charge of $____ per hour for any work which follows a deposition, including expert testimony in civil procedures, courtroom appearances, and review or preparation of documents relating to courtroom testimony, and any time spent traveling to or from such procedures or while waiting on-call for such procedures to take place.

I acknowledge that the financial responsibility for paying such fees to the undersigned psychologist will be mine and not that of my client. I promise to make immediate payment in full to the undersigned psychologist upon my receipt of his or her bill for any services rendered.

This _____ day of _____.

_____

ATTORNEY'S SIGNATURE

_____

PSYCHOLOGIST'S SIGNATURE

Sworn to and subscribed
before me this _____
day of _____.

_____

NOTARY PUBLIC'S SIGNATURE

My commission expires:_____

APPENDIX F

STATEMENT OF UNDERSTANDING FOR UNAUTHORIZED SERVICES AND FOR SERVICES BEYOND MEDICAL NECESSITY

Managed care companies (MCCs) and health maintenance organizations (HMOs) are designed to cover crisis stabilization services which they consider *medically necessary*. They do not authorize or pay for counseling or psychotherapy beyond their definition of "medical necessity." They also do not authorize or pay for personality or psychological testing services which they do not consider "medically necessary."

The undersigned psychologist cannot predict or control how many sessions or services will be authorized by your managed care company. Surveys and experience with some managed care companies suggest that they authorize an average of approximately six crisis-oriented psychotherapy sessions, although your particular company may approve more or less than six sessions. Most managed care companies will also allow you to receive counseling, psychotherapy sessions, psychological testing, or other services beyond the point of *medical necessity*, although you will be financially responsible for those additional services.

Statement of Financial Responsibility

I have requested services by the undersigned psychologist that are either not authorized or paid for by my insurance or managed care company.

I have been informed by the undersigned psychologist that my managed care company is not likely to authorize payment for services beyond their definition of medical necessity.

I understand and I agree that I am personally and fully responsible for payment of these services at the time services are rendered to me.

_____   _____
PATIENT'S SIGNATURE   DATE

_____   _____
PSYCHOLOGIST'S SIGNATURE   DATE

_____   _____
GUARANTOR'S SIGNATURE   DATE

APPENDIX G

RECORD OF CONVERSATION

WITH: _____ FILE: _____

DATE: _____ PHONE: _____

_____

_____

_____

_____

_____

_____

_____

_____

_____

_____

_____

_____

_____

_____

REFERENCES

Alfidi, R. J. (1975). Controversy, alternatives, and decisions in complying with the legal doctrine of informed consent. *Radiology, 114*, 231-234.

American Home Assurance Company. (1990). *Psychologist's Professional Liability Policy*. New York: Author.

American Medical Association. (1997). *Physicians' Current Procedural Terminology*. Chicago: Author.

American Psychiatric Association. (1993). *The Principles of Medical Ethics With Annotations Especially Applicable to Psychiatry*. Washington, DC: Author.

American Psychological Association. (1987). *General Guidelines for Providers of Psychological Services*. Washington, DC: Author.

American Psychological Association. (1992). Ethical Principles of Psychologists and Code of Conduct. *American Psychologist, 47*, 1597-1611.

American Psychological Association. (1994). Guidelines for child custody evaluations in divorce proceedings. *American Psychologist, 49*(7), 677-680.

American Psychological Association. (1996). Rules and procedures. Ethics Committee of the American Psychological Association. *American Psychologist, 51*(5), 529-548.

American Psychological Association Insurance Trust, Professional Liability Insurance Program. (1996). *Professional Liability Insurance for Psychologists. Application Form*. Des Moines, IA: Author.

Andrews, L. B. (1984). Informed consent statutes and the decision-making process. *Journal of Legal Medicine, 5,* 163-217.

Barnett, J. E. (1997). How to avoid malpractice. *The Independent Practitioner, 17*(1), 20-22.

Bennett, B., Harris, E., & Remar, R. (1995, April 22-23). *Risk Management.* Workshop presented at the annual meeting of the Georgia Psychological Association, Atlanta, GA.

Bennett, B., Harris, E., & Remar, R. (1996, May 30). *Ethics and Risk Management.* Workshop presented at the annual meeting of the Georgia Psychological Association, Savannah, GA.

Bennett, B., Harris, E., & Remar, R. (1997, May 15). *Ethics and Risk Management.* Workshop presented at the annual meeting of the Georgia Psychological Association, Emory Conference Center, Atlanta, GA.

Bersoff, D. N. (1995). *Ethical Conflicts in Psychology.* Washington, DC: American Psychological Association.

Bridge, P. J., & Bascue, L. O. (1988). A record form for psychotherapy supervisors. In P. A. Keller & S. R. Heyman (Eds.), *Innovations in Clinical Practice: A Source Book* (Vol. 7, pp. 331-336), Sarasota, FL: Professional Resource Exchange.

Buchanan, W. (1997, January 17). *Mental Health Ethics and Georgia Law.* Continuing education workshop sponsored by the Georgia School of Professional Psychology at Georgia State University, North Campus, Atlanta, GA.

Canadian Psychological Association. (1991). *Canadian Code of Ethics for Psychologists, Revised 1991.* Ottawa, Ontario, Canada: Author.

Canter, M. B., Bennett, B. E., Jones, S. E., & Nagy, T. F. (1994). *Ethics for Psychologists: A Commentary on the APA Ethics Code.* Washington, DC: American Psychological Association.

Canterbury v. Spence, 464 F.2d 772, 789 (D.C. Cir. 1972).

Clites v. Iowa, No. 46247 (Pottawattamie County, Iowa, 1980).

Committee on Ethical Guidelines for Forensic Psychologists. (1991). Specialty Guidelines for Forensic Psychologists. *Law and Human Behavior, 15*(6), 655-665.

Committee on Professional Practice and Standards. (1993). Record keeping guidelines. *American Psychologist, 48*(9), 984-986.

Crawford, R. J. (1994). *Avoiding Counselor Malpractice*. Alexandria, VA: American Counseling Association.

DeFilippis, N. A., Wilbanks, M., Doverspike, W. F., Dsurney, J., & Bridges, J. D. (1997, February 14). *Everyday Considerations in Treating Litigating Clients: An Ethical Balancing Act*. Workshop presented at the Georgia Psychological Association Central Office, Atlanta, GA.

Department of Health and Human Services. (1987). Confidentiality of alcohol and drug abuse patient records. *Federal Register*, *42*, 21796-21814.

Doverspike, W. F. (1995). Some survival tips for dealing with insurance companies and managed care. In L. VandeCreek, S. Knapp, & T. L. Jackson (Eds.), *Innovations in Clinical Practice: A Source Book* (Vol. 14, pp. 255-262). Sarasota, FL: Professional Resource Press.

Doverspike, W. F. (1996a). Informed consent for psychological services: Clinical services. *Georgia Psychologist*, *50*(2), 56-58.

Doverspike, W. F. (1996b). Informed consent for psychological services: Financial responsibility. *Georgia Psychologist*, *50(*4), 24-26.

Doverspike, W. F. (1997a). Putting ethics into practice: Some personal reflections. *Georgia Psychologist*, *51*(1), 22-24.

Doverspike, W. F. (1997b). Informed consent forms. In L. VandeCreek, S. Knapp, & T. L. Jackson (Eds.), *Innovations in Clinical Practice: A Source Book* (Vol. 15, pp. 201-214). Sarasota, FL: Professional Resource Press.

Doverspike, W. F. (1997c). Ethical decision making: Doing the next right thing. *Georgia Psychologist*, *51*(2), 29-33.

Doverspike, W. F. (1999a). Ethical risk management: Protecting your practice. In L. VandeCreek & T. L. Jackson (Eds.), *Innovations in Clinical Practice: A Source Book* (Vol. 17, pp. 269-278). Sarasota, FL: Professional Resource Press.

Doverspike, W. F. (1999b). How to respond to an ethics complaint. *Georgia Psychologist*, *53*(2), 25-27.

Eberlein, L. (1987). Introducing ethics to beginning psychologists: A problem-solving approach. *Professional Psychology: Research and Practice*, *18*, 353-359.

Eyde, L. D., & Quaintance, M. K. (1988). Ethical issues and cases in the practice of personnel psychology. *Professional Psychology: Research and Practice*, *19*, 148-154.

Florida Statutes. State of Florida Chapter 21U-15.004.

Gabbard, G., & Pope, K. (1988). Sexual intimacies after termination: Clinical, ethical, and legal aspects. *The Independent Practitioner, 8*(2), 21-26.

Georgia Psychological Association. (1996). *Rules and Procedures of The Georgia Psychological Association Ethics Committee (Revised June 18, 1996).* Atlanta, GA: Author.

Georgia State Board of Examiners of Psychologists, Laws. §§43-1-1 to 43-39-20. (eff. August 31, 1997).

Georgia State Board of Examiners of Psychologists, Rules. §§510-1 to 510-10. (eff. March 9, 1999).

Gerts, B. (1981). *The Moral Rules.* New York: Ballantine.

Golden, L. (1992). Dual role relationships in private practice. In B. Herlihy & C. Corey (Eds.), *Dual Relationships in Counseling* (pp. 130-133). Alexandria, VA: American Association for Counseling and Development.

Gottlieb, M. C. (1993). Avoiding exploitive dual relationships: A decision-making model. *Psychotherapy, 30,* 41-47.

Gutheil, T. G. (1980). Paranoia and progress notes: A guide to forensically informed psychiatric record keeping. *Hospital and Community Psychiatry, 13,* 479-482.

Haas, L. J., & Malouf, J. L. (1995). *Keeping Up the Good Work: A Practitioner's Guide to Mental Health Ethics* (2nd ed.). Sarasota, FL: Professional Resource Press.

Handelsman, M. M., & Galvin, M. D. (1988). Facilitating informed consent for outpatient psychotherapy: A suggested written format. *Professional Psychology: Research and Practice, 19,* 223-225.

Harris, E., & Remar, R. (1998, June 5). *Ethics and Risk Management.* Workshop presented to the Georgia Psychological Association, Fairfield Inn, Atlanta, GA.

Herlihy, B., & Corey, G. (1996). *American Counseling Association Ethical Standards Casebook* (5th ed.). Alexandria, VA: American Counseling Association.

Herman, J. L., Gartrell, N., Olarte, S., Feldstein, M., & Localio, R. (1987). Psychiatrist-patient sexual contact: Results of a national survey, II: Psychiatrists' attitudes. *American Journal of Psychiatry, 144,* 164-169.

Hill, M., Glaser, K., & Harden, J. (1995). A feminist model for ethical decision making. In E. J. Rave & C. C. Larsen (Eds.),

Ethical Decision Making in Therapy: Feminist Perspectives (pp. 18-37). New York: Guilford.

Huxley, A. L. (1956). *Reader's Digest.* New York: Reader's Digest.

Keith-Spiegel, P., & Koocher, G. P. (1985). *Ethics in Psychology: Professional Standards and Cases.* New York: Random House.

Kitchener, K. S. (1984). Intuition, critical evaluation and ethical principles: The foundation for ethical decisions in counseling psychology. *The Counseling Psychologist, 12,* 306-310.

Knapp, S., & VandeCreek, L. (1997). Questions and answers about clinical supervision. In L. VandeCreek, S. Knapp, & T. L. Jackson (Eds.), *Innovations in Clinical Practice: A Source Book* (Vol. 15, pp. 189-197). Professional Resource Press.

Koocher, G. P., & Keith-Spiegel, P. (1998). *Ethics in Psychology: Professional Standards and Cases* (2nd ed.). New York: Oxford Textbooks in Clinical Psychology.

Kovacs, A. L. (1984). The increasing malpractice exposure of psychologists. *The Independent Practitioner, 4*(2), 12-14.

Meara, N. M., Schmidt, L. D., & Day, J. D. (1996). Principles and virtues: A foundation for ethical decisions, policies, and character. *The Counseling Psychologist, 24*(1), 4-77.

Moore, G. (1900). *The Bending of the Bough: A Comedy in Five Acts,* Act IV. New York: H. S. Stone.

Morris, R. J. (1997). Child custody evaluations: A risky business. *Register Report, 23*(1), 6-7.

Moye, J., & Brown, E. (1995). Postdoctoral training in geropsychology: Guidelines for formal programs and continuing education. *Professional Psychology: Research and Practice, 26*(6), 591-597.

Official Code of Georgia Annotated (§§*43-1-19(a), 43-1-25, 43-39-5(d), 43-39-13.). Rules of the State Board of Examiners of Psychologists, Chapter 510-3-.12 (1a) Violations of Applicable Statutes* (Original Rule entitled "Violations of Law" adopted F. Jul 27, 1994; eff. Aug. 16, 1994).

Piazza, N. J., & Baruth, N. E. (1990). Client record guidelines. *Journal of Counseling and Development, 68,* 313-316.

Piazza, N. J., & Yeager, R. D. (1991). The client record as a tool for risk management. In P. A. Keller & S. R. Heyman (Eds.), *Innovations in Clinical Practice: A Source Book* (Vol.

10, pp. 341-352). Sarasota, FL: Professional Resource Exchange.

Pope, K. S. (1986). New trends in malpractice cases and changes in APA liability insurance. *The Independent Practitioner,* 6(4), 23-26.

Pope, K. S. (1989a, February 4). *Reducing Risks of Ethical Violations and Malpractice.* Workshop presented at the Georgia Psychological Association Midwinter Conference, Mariner's Inn, Hilton Head Island, SC.

Pope, K. S. (1989b). Malpractice suits, licensing disciplinary actions, and ethics cases: Frequencies, causes, and costs. *The Independent Practitioner,* 9(1), 22-26.

Pope, K. S., Tabachnick, B. G., & Keith-Spiegel, P. (1987). Ethics of practice: The beliefs and behaviors of psychologists as therapists. *American Psychologist, 42,* 993-1006.

Pope, K. S., & Vasquez, M. J. T. (1991). *Ethics in Psychotherapy and Counseling: A Practical Guide for Psychologists.* San Francisco: Jossey-Bass.

Remar, R. B., & Hubert, R. N. (1996). *Law & Mental Health Professionals: Georgia.* Washington, DC: American Psychological Association.

Reports of the INS – Division 40 Task Force on Education, Accreditation, and Credentialing. (1987). *The Clinical Neuropsychologist, 1*(1), 29-34.

Schlosser, B., & Tower, R. B. (1991). Office policies for assessment services. In P. A. Keller & S. R. Heyman (Eds.), *Innovations in Clinical Practice* (Vol. 10, pp. 393-411). Sarasota, FL: Professional Resource Exchange.

Shapiro, D. (1994, January 15). *Ethical Constraints in an Age of Litigation.* Workshop presented at the Midwinter Conference, Georgia Psychological Association, Ashville, NC.

Sinclair, C., Poizner, S., Gilmour-Barrett, K., & Randall, D. (1987). The development of a code of ethics for Canadian psychologists. *Canadian Psychology, 28,* 1-8.

Smith, R., Graves, J., Hall, J., & Paddock, J. (1994, November 17). *Therapeutic Malpractice.* Continuing education workshop presented in Atlanta, GA.

Soisson, E. L., VandeCreek, L., & Knapp, S. (1987). Thorough record keeping: A good defense in a litigious era. *Professional Psychology: Research and Practice, 19*(5), 498-502.

Stadler, H. A. (1986). Making hard choices: Clarifying controversial ethical issues. *Journal of Counseling and Human Development, 19,* 1-10.

Stoltenberg, C. D., & Delworth, U. (1987). *Supervising Counselors and Therapists.* San Francisco: Jossey-Bass.

Stromberg, C. D., & Dellinger, A. (1993). Malpractice and other professional liability. *The Psychologist's Legal Update, 3.* Washington, DC: National Register of Health Service Providers in Psychology.

Stromberg, C. D., Haggarty, D. J., Leibenluft, R. F., McMillian, M. H., Mishkin, B., Rubin, B. L., & Trilling, H. R. (1988). *The Psychologist's Legal Handbook.* Washington, DC: The Council for the National Register of Health Service Providers in Psychology.

Sullivan, T., Martin, W. L., Jr., & Handelsman, M. (1993). Practical benefits of an informed-consent procedure: An empirical investigation. *Professional Psychology: Research and Practice, 24,* 160-163.

Sutton, W. A. (1986, November 1). *Malpractice Issues in a Hospital Setting.* Workshop presented at CPC Parkwood Hospital, Atlanta, GA.

Switankowsky, I. S. (1998). *A New Paradigm for Informed Consent.* Lanham, MD: University Press of America.

Twain, M. (1901, February 16). *To the Young People's Society.* Brooklyn, NY: Greenpoint Presbyterian Church.

Tymchuk, A. J. (1986). Guidelines for ethical decision making. *Canadian Psychology, 27,* 36-43.

Van Hoose, W. H., & Paradise, L. V. (1979). *Ethics in Counseling and Psychotherapy: Perspectives in Issues and Decision Making.* Cranston, RI: Carroll Press.

Weiner, B. A., & Wettstein, R. M. (1993). *Legal Issues in Mental Health Care.* New York: Plenum.

Woody, R. H. (1988). *Fifty Ways to Avoid Malpractice: A Guidebook for Mental Health Professionals.* Sarasota, FL: Professional Resource Exchange.

Younggren, J. N. (1995). Informed consent: Simply a reminder. *Register Report, 21,* 6-7.

SUBJECT INDEX

Add A Colleague To Our Mailing List . . .

If you would like us to send our latest catalog to one of your colleagues, please return this form.

Name:_____
(Please Print)

Address:_____

Address:_____

City/State/Zip:_____
This is ❏ home ❏ office

Telephone:(_____)_____

This person is a:

_____ Psychologist   _____ Mental Health Counselor
_____ Psychiatrist   _____ Marriage and Family Therapist
_____ School Psychologist   _____ Not in Mental Health Field
_____ Clinical Social Worker   _____ Other:_____

Name of person completing this form:_____

◆   ◆   ◆

Professional Resource Press
P.O. Box 15560
Sarasota, FL 34277-1560

Telephone: 800-443-3364
FAX: 941-343-9201
E-mail: mail@prpress.com
Website: http://www.prpress.com

Add A Colleague To Our Mailing List . . .

If you would like us to send our latest catalog to one of your colleagues, please return this form.

Name:_____
(Please Print)

Address:_____

Address:_____

City/State/Zip:_____
This is ❐ home ❐ office

Telephone:(_____)_____

This person is a:

_____ Psychologist   _____ Mental Health Counselor
_____ Psychiatrist   _____ Marriage and Family Therapist
_____ School Psychologist   _____ Not in Mental Health Field
_____ Clinical Social Worker   _____ Other:_____

Name of person completing this form:_____

◆   ◆   ◆

Professional Resource Press
P.O. Box 15560
Sarasota, FL 34277-1560

Telephone: 800-443-3364
FAX: 941-343-9201
E-mail: mail@prpress.com
Website: http://www.prpress.com

ERM/7/99